The Media

ISSUES

Volume 69

Editor

Craig Donnellan

Independence

Educational Publishers
Cambridge

First published by Independence
PO Box 295
Cambridge CB1 3XP
England

British Library Cataloguing in Publication Data
The Media – (Issues Series)
I. Donnellan, Craig II. Series
302.2'3

ISBN 1 86168 251 4

Printed in Great Britain
MWL Print Group Ltd

Typeset by
Claire Boyd

Cover
The illustration on the front cover is by
Pumpkin House.

CONTENTS

Chapter One: Social Effects

Chapter Two: Regulation and Ownership

Introduction

The Media is the sixty-ninth volume in the **Issues** series. The aim of this series is to offer up-to-date information about important issues in our world.

The Media examines the role of the media in our society and the rules and regulations concerning the media.

The information comes from a wide variety of sources and includes:
Government reports and statistics
Newspaper reports and features
Magazine articles and surveys
Web site material
Literature from lobby groups
and charitable organisations.

It is hoped that, as you read about the many aspects of the issues explored in this book, you will critically evaluate the information presented. It is important that you decide whether you are being presented with facts or opinions. Does the writer give a biased or an unbiased report? If an opinion is being expressed, do you agree with the writer?

The Media offers a useful starting-point for those who need convenient access to information about the many issues involved. However, it is only a starting-point. At the back of the book is a list of organisations which you may want to contact for further information.

*****

The public's view

Viewers say news is the public service priority according to ITC and BSC research

News is the most important programme genre to television viewers, both as a vital component of public service broadcasting and in terms of personal interest, according to new research by the Independent Television Commission and the Broadcasting Standards Commission, published on 12 March 2003.

The Public's View 2002 reveals that 93% of respondents consider it essential (or very important) that BBC1 and ITV1 continue to show news programmes, and the same number said they are interested in watching such programmes.

There has been a significant increase in the number of people who regard television as their main source of world news: 79% in 2002, compared with 66% in 2001. By contrast, 9% of respondents named newspapers, down from 16% in 2001. Tabloid readers were more likely than broadsheet readers to use television as their main source of world news.

Television also remains the dominant medium for national and regional news. When asked which source of news they trusted to be the most fair and unbiased, 70% said television, compared with 14% for radio and 6% for (any) newspaper. Most respondents (89%) thought that television news was accurate all, or most of, the time.

Concerns about television standards in general, however, remain high – on a level with those observed in 2001, with 47% of respondents thinking standards had got worse (compared with 28% in 2000). The number of repeats on television was the major source of complaint (mentioned by 47%), followed by concern about 'not enough quality' (18%, an increase of 6% since 2001). A new cause for concern among respondents was the perception of intrusion into people's lives: 61% thought there was too much, making it a greater concern than too much sexual content (44%), swearing (56%) or violence (58%).

The Public's View 2002 covers a wide range of issues, from the changes in media technology ownership in the home, viewing habits and preferences, attitudes towards regulation and causes of offence to the importance of different programme genres, views on television advertising, and the use of radio and the internet.

Access to a whole range of communications and home entertainment technologies continues to grow strongly. The research shows that personal computer ownership, in particular, is growing, with nearly half of respondents having a PC at home: 46% compared with 39% in 2001. Almost half of all homes with children now have internet access. Frequency of access is also rising: in 39% of internet homes, it is accessed daily, or almost every day.

Despite the demise of ITV Digital, penetration of digital television increased slightly, with 41% of respondents now having digital services (51% have multi-channel television). Many of the newer services available are being used by multichannel viewers, with half watching pay-per-view content, usually films. Interactive services on digital television are still seeking a wider market – 66% of those with

access said they never used them, compared with 62% in 2001.

'The 2002 survey underlines the importance of access to independent, impartial news programmes on popular channels,' says ITC Chief Executive Patricia Hodgson. 'The public is telling us that this is the most important public service television can offer them.'

Paul Bolt, Director of the BSC, added: 'This survey shows that while a large proportion of the public now has access to a wide range of home entertainment services, many people still have real concerns about standards on the familiar terrestrial channels'.

There were some significant national variations in ownership of new technology. Respondents in England had the highest level of access to PCs: 47%, compared with 41% for Wales, 40% for Scotland and 36% for Northern Ireland. The difference for internet access was even sharper: England 44%, Scotland 35%, Wales 31% and Northern Ireland 24%. Respondents from Northern Ireland were also less likely to have technology such as teletext, stereo sound, video games and DVD. Ownership of video recorders was highest in Scotland: 93%, compared with 90% for N. Ireland, 87% for England and 82% for Wales.

Viewing habits and preferences

BBC1 overtook ITV1 as the channel that most viewers would want if they could have only one channel (34% for BBC1, compared with 27% for ITV1, 7% for Channel 4 and BBC2, and 3% for Five. Sky Sports and Sky One were nominated by 4% each). BBC1 was also judged to be the most-watched channel by 34% of respondents, compared with 30% for ITV1, and 6% for Channel 4 and BBC2. Viewers with digital television were positive about the benefits of interactive services in theory, but usage fell slightly, with 15% saying they used such services at least once a week, compared with 19% in 2001. Those saying they never used such services rose from 62% to 66%. Interest in acquiring multichannel television remained steady: 27% claimed to be interested.

Regulation

Most respondents (74%) think the main aim of programme content regulation is to protect children and young people; a further 23% believe it is for the protection of all viewers. The majority (55%) thinks there is about the right amount of regulation on ITV1, Channels 4 and Five, while 65% thought that the BBC was regulated sufficiently. Multichannel viewers were also satisfied with the amount of regulation on channels other than the BBC and 3-5. For advertising, 65% thought the amount of regulation was about right for ITV1, Channels 4 and Five, a view echoed by multichannel viewers for the additional channels.

Sources of news

When asked which source of news was most trusted (television, newspapers or radio), 70% named television, almost the same number as had named television as their main source of UK news. Television was also the dominant medium for giving information about world news, with 79% citing it in 2002, compared with 66% in 2001 – an increase which may be due, in part, to the events of 11 September 2001 (which took place after the fieldwork for the 2001 study was completed). Television retained its dominance even as a source of local news: 48% of respondents said it was their main source of information on local news, compared with 32% for newspapers.

Quality and standards within programmes

Viewers continue to be concerned about quality and standards in general on television, with 47% of respondents thinking that programmes had got worse (older people were far more likely than younger ones to take this view). Giving unprompted responses for why this might be, the most common complaint (as in previous years) was about the number of repeats, mentioned by 47%. A significant area of concern this year was media intrusion into people's private lives; 61% of respondents said there was too much. There was also unprompted concern about issues such as offensive language, violence and sex (24%,

23% and 21% respectively). When it came to any perceived political bias, 68% said they did not see evidence of any one party being favoured by any channel. BBC1 and BBC2 were the most likely to be named as being politically biased, (16% and 6% thought this was the case, respectively), and of those who did perceive bias, most said it was in favour of the Labour Party. News and wildlife programmes were judged most likely to be factually accurate (by 89% of respondents), more so than current affairs (69%), dramatised reconstructions (68%) or documentaries (59%).

Offence and acceptability

Asked if they personally saw things they found offensive on television, 42% of respondents said they did, but there were significant differences among age groups, with only 17% of younger viewers saying they had been offended, compared with 77% of the respondents over 75. Channel 4, followed by ITV, was the channel most likely to be named as the source of offence among terrestrial channels (53% and 45% respectively). Asked about five particular possible causes of offence, 61% thought there was too much media intrusion on television, compared with 58% saying there was too much violence, 56% too much swearing and 44% too much sex. Asked for their most memorable television moment, 44% mentioned the coverage of the US terrorist attacks of the previous year, 11 September 2001. This was the largest number of mentions for any event since the death and funeral of Diana, Princess of Wales (cited by 61% of respondents in the 1998 survey).

Protection of children

There was a slight change in attitudes towards self-regulation in 2002, with 65% of respondents saying that parents should be mainly responsible for what their children watched, and 8% saying the main responsibility lay with broadcasters (compared with 62% and 10% in 2001). This fits with the levels of self-regulation exercised by respondents, the majority of whom said they switched off or over if they saw something they found offensive. Awareness of the family viewing policy (the Watershed) remained almost universal at 97%, and 64% of all respondents considered this to be the right time. Older viewers (45-74-year-olds) and parents of children aged 10-15 were the most likely to say that 9pm was too early.

Programme genres

As in previous years, when asked which programme genres were the most important to them personally, news had the highest rating (93% said it was of interest), followed by factual programmes (84%), drama (81%), entertainment (77%) and regional programmes (71%). There was least interest in religious programming (24%). Children's programming was not necessarily of personal interest to respondents, but when asked about the kind of programmes they thought that BBC1 and ITV1 should carry, as part of their public service remit, it was the third most popular genre. Children's and factual programmes were mentioned by 65%, current affairs by 66% and news by 93%. Levels of satisfaction with the range of choice available increased: 45% of respondents said that the channels they received gave them all the choice they wanted, compared with 41% in 2001.

Attitudes to advertising

There were few changes in attitudes since last year's survey, with humour still being the quality most liked about advertising, and the interruption to programmes the most disliked feature. There was an increase of awareness in other forms of promotional messages such as programme sponsorship, trailers and channel promotions. The majority of respondents (55%) thought the current amounts of advertising on terrestrial television were about right, although fewer multichannel viewers (47%) were satisfied with the amount of advertising on non-terrestrial channels. There was a higher tolerance for the idea of more sponsorship and trailers/channel promotions on terrestrial television than there was for more advertising. Levels of offence at advertising were low: 81% had not encountered an offensive advertisement.

Radio

Most respondents (57%) said that they listened to the radio every day and 87% said they have not heard anything that offended them. The heaviest amount of listening is in the older age groups, social groups ABC1 and by people in Wales. Only 10% of listeners had accessed radio services via their television sets, with younger people (17%), multichannel (19%) and digital viewers (22%) and non-white respondents (22%) more likely to do so.

The internet

Internet access increased in 2002 to 52% of respondents (47% in 2001), the majority accessing it at home. Those most likely to have internet access were people in social grades AB (71%), those aged 16-24 (76%) and non-white people (78%). Email remains the most popular reason for using the internet (64%), followed by research and looking for information (mentioned by 58%), then travel and holiday information (26%) and information for shopping (24%). Use of the internet for school, college or university work has fallen, from 20% in 2001 to 10% in 2002. Only 8% of internet users have accessed it via their television sets at home, but 2% said they used this method often. Knowledge of controlling internet access continues to grow, with over half of respondents having heard of more than one such control. Among parents, 33% said they used some kind of filtering tool.

■ Copies of *The Public's View 2002* are available for £7.50 from the ITC Viewer Relations Unit, telephone 020 7255 3000. Alternatively, the text can be downloaded free of charge from the ITC and BSC websites at www.itc.org.uk and www.bsc.org.uk

The Public's View 2002 is the 32nd in a series of annual surveys commissioned by the Independent Television Commission and the bodies that preceded it to track changes in public attitudes towards broadcasting and the take-up of new technologies in the home. In 2001, the research was commissioned jointly for the first time with the Broadcasting Standards Commission, and included new questions to reflect their remit, including questions on radio.

■ The above information is from the Broadcasting Standards Commission's web site which can be found at www.bsc.org.uk

© Broadcasting Standards Commission/ Independent Television Commission

Uses of the media

Different people use the media for different reasons. How much does each apply?

	Applies a lot	Quite a lot	A little	Does not apply at all
Lets me follow important events and crises	46%	41%	11%	2%
Keeps me in touch with what's going on in Britain	42%	46%	10%	2%
Keeps me in touch with what's going on in other parts of the world	41%	45%	12%	2%
Keeps me in touch with local issues	21%	46%	26%	7%
Lets me see how society works	18%	40%	35%	8%
Gives me a good laugh	17%	34%	38%	11%
Shows what people in authority are really like	15%	35%	35%	15%
Helps me relax	15%	32%	33%	20%
Keeps me company	14%	25%	36%	24%
Cheers me up	12%	31%	38%	20%
Helps me feel part of my community	11%	24%	41%	24%
Shows me how ordinary people live	10%	29%	46%	16%
Tells me about famous people I am interested in	9%	30%	43%	18%
Tells me about people I admire	7%	27%	46%	20%
Gives advice on personal problems	5%	14%	40%	41%

Source: The Public Interest, the Media and Privacy, BBC, BSC, Independent Committee for the Supervision of Standards of Telephone Information Services, ITC, Institute for Public Policy Research and The Radio Authority

TV taste and decency in decline, say viewers

By Chris Hastings, Media Correspondent

More than half of the British public believe that standards of taste and decency on television are getting worse, according to a new survey by the broadcasting industry's watchdogs.

The survey, to be published by the Broadcasting Standards Commission and the Independent Television Commission, will also disclose that a third of people think that the quality of programmes is deteriorating.

The prime concern of the 1,100 viewers questioned for the survey was the level of violence, which was cited by more than half those who complained about programme content. Explicit sex and bad language also prompted a large number of protests. Overall, more than 40 per cent of viewers said that they had been offended by material screened during the last year.

Kim Howells, the Government's minister for broadcasting, expressed alarm at the findings and accused the television channels of screening 'gratuitous' material which had 'a corroding effect on the soul'. He urged the television channels to reassess their content.

'I think people are growing increasingly worried about the levels of violence in television,' he said. 'Broadcasters including the BBC need to ask themselves what they are trying to achieve with programmes like these. I think a lot of the content has a corroding effect on the soul.

'I am particularly worried about the violence which would seem to have no relation to real life. A lot of it is simply gratuitous and it plays to the lowest common denominator.'

Among the shows attracting criticism in the survey are *EastEnders* and *Coronation Street*, both of which have used violent storylines to attract huge ratings in recent months, despite being broadcast before the 9pm watershed.

Fifty-six per cent of viewers also complained about the use of bad language in programmes, such as *Jamie's Kitchen* on Channel Four, which was presented by Jamie Oliver, the television chef.

The explicit sexual content of programmes such as *Tipping the Velvet*, the lesbian drama shown on BBC2 last year, which was cited by 44 per cent of complainants, attracted similarly widespread criticism.

Viewers are also unhappy with reality television shows such as Channel Four's *Big Brother*, with more than two-thirds of complainants saying that they featured 'excessive intrusion' into people's private lives.

In a section on viewers' perceptions of taste and decency, which was included in the annual survey for the first time, 55 per cent said that standards had declined. Only five per cent said that there had been an improvement.

Although the survey will show that Channel Four remains Britain's most 'offensive' channel, attracting 53 per cent of all complaints, there is a significant increase in concern about BBC1's output. More than 37 per cent of those who expressed concern about programmes claimed that the channel had breached guidelines on taste and decency.

Forty-four per cent of those who expressed concern about BBC1 were worried about the levels of violence on the channel. There was also an increased number of complaints about offensive language on BBC1 programmes, and about sexual content.

The survey reveals that women, older viewers and the readers of broadsheet newspapers are most likely to be offended by broadcast material. The majority of complaints about sex and violence came from older viewers, with more than 70 per cent of viewers aged 75 and over saying that they had been offended by something on television.

Younger people were more likely to be concerned about the intrusive nature of programmes, with 58 per cent of viewers aged between 16 and 44 naming this as a problem.

John Beyer, the director of Media Watch UK, a pressure group that campaigns for tighter controls on television, expressed similar sentiments.

He said: 'This represents a very significant increase in the number of people registering concerns and I welcome that. The question now is what will the broadcasters do about it.'

Mr Beyer said that he believed broadcasters were deliberately flouting guidelines in the run-up to the establishment of Ofcom, the Government's new broadcasting watchdog, which begins operating in December.

A spokesman for Channel Four said: 'British television is very strictly controlled by the regulator and we take the watershed very seriously. We have a good relationship with

the regulator and a good record on compliance.'

A BBC spokesman admitted that there had been a slight increase in the number of complaints that it had received. She insisted, however, that complaints

about sex and violence accounted for only a small proportion of the concerns raised by viewers.

The Broadcasting Standards Commission was established in 1996 as the statutory watchdog covering standards and fairness on television and radio, including text, cable and digital services. It is funded by the Government. The ITC is funded by the commercial television sector: it licenses commercial television stations, which gives it a regulatory function by ensuring that broadcasters stick to the terms of their licences.

© Telegraph Group Limited, London 2003

Children's TV

Amount of children's TV programming has tripled since 1997

There are now more children's programmes on television than at any time over the last eleven years, according to new research published by the Broadcasting Standards Commission and the Independent Television Commission.

The report also shows that the most balanced and diverse line-up of programming continues to be provided by the terrestrial television networks. This included factual, drama, light entertainment and pre-school programming. The mainstay of children's programming on all channels is animation, which includes, but not exclusively, cartoons (for example, Bob the Builder, Thomas and Friends and Fireman Sam).

Results from What Children Watch, an analysis of children's programming provision between 1997-2001, and children's views on what they watch, shows that the increase in the amount of provision of children's programmes over the last five years is derived from the launch of Channel 5 (FIVE), and from the introduction of new dedicated satellite and cable channels. Children in multichannel homes are now able to tune in to dedicated children's channels at any

time of day. The research period predated the introduction of the new CBBC and CBeebies channels, which has further increased the choice available.

There are differences in the range of genres offered to children between the services. The provision of drama on terrestrial television networks is more stable than some of the other genres, with little change across the period sampled. On the dedicated channels, however, there was a steep decline in drama in 2001. Factual programming (such as Newsround, Blue Peter, How II and Art Attack) is almost absent from the dedicated channels, while light entertainment (such as Kenan & Kel, Saved by the Bell and The Saturday Show) takes a significant proportion of the share across all platforms. Pre-

The television landscape has changed significantly over recent times – part of this change has been a result of the way in which younger viewers are consuming media

school programming (such as Tele-tubbies, Sesame Street, the Hoobs and PB Bear & Friends) featured well on the dedicated channels, and an increase in provision was noted on the analogue terrestrial television platform.

The television landscape has changed significantly over recent times – part of this change has been a result of the way in which younger viewers are consuming media. Households with children contain a wider range of in-home entertainment than child-free households and are more likely to be 'early adopters' of such equipment. 59% of people with children have access to multichannel television, compared with 46% of households without children.

The report found that children in multichannel homes watch significantly more television than their terrestrial-only counterparts (on average 35 minutes more per day). Animation of all types accounted for over half the time children in multichannel homes spent viewing television. However, the amount of time they spend specifically viewing 'children's programmes' is comparable with those living in terrestrial-only homes.

Interviews with children underscored the findings that television is of significant importance in their lives. Most homes have more than one television set and most of the children interviewed have a set in their bedroom. The survey reports that television is a prime source of entertainment, if not a preferred activity. The children interviewed watch at all times; very often the television is on, even if not actively watched.

Many of the children who live in analogue terrestrial-only homes say that they have been exposed to the other channels and services and have some knowledge of them. Children in multichannel homes are more demanding of their television schedules, expecting a large number of different programmes, constantly changing. Those in analogue terrestrial-only homes are more aware of the scheduling of their favourite programmes and the channel on which they are broadcast.

The issue of programme origination was raised with children but was not found to be of significant interest, although many spoke of their enjoyment of US-produced programming. Parents, especially those

in analogue terrestrial-only homes, are particularly keen that UK-originated programming should be available for their children to watch. They feel it is more authentic and culturally relevant. Some feel that it has more of an educational value.

Parents also feel that it is important to retain children's programming on analogue terrestrial channels, despite the alternative sources available on cable and satellite channels. Those parents in terrestrial-only homes say they would resent being forced to pay for additional services in order for their children to have something to watch.

On behalf of the sponsors of the research, Andrea Millwood

Hargrave, Director of the Joint Research Programme, BSC and ITC, said: 'This research, a continuation of work first undertaken by the BSC over 6 years ago, shows that despite the number and popularity of the newer, specialist channels, the range of programming available is not as diverse as it could be. The terrestrial free-to-air channels continue to provide the greatest balance of diverse content, especially of factual and drama output. Television remains one of the most important sources of leisure entertainment for children and, with 59% penetration of multichannel television in homes with children, they have become more demanding of the quality of programmes on offer.'

Notes

1. *What Children Watch* is an analysis of children's programming provision between 1997 and 2001, and children's views of what they watch. It updates the survey last undertaken seven years ago by Messenger Davies, M, & Corbett, B 'The Provision of Children's Television in Britain: 1992-1996'. The qualitative research among children (42 aged 6-12) and 50 parents (12 dads and 38 mums)

Top children's television programmes

The top television programmes, across the entire children audience in 2002

Programme	Genre	Channel	Viewers, %	000's viewers
EastEnders	Drama: Soaps UK	BBC1	25.8	2371
Pop Idol Live Final	Entertainment: Family Shows	ITV1	24.1	2218
Only Fools and Horses	Entertainment: Situation Comedy UK	BBC1	22.7	2087
A Bug's Life	Films: Cinema US	BBC1	21.1	1942
The Mummy	Films: Cinema US	BBC1	20.8	1919
World Cup 2002: Argentina vs. England	Sport: Football	BBC1	20.7	1910
Coronation Street	Drama: Soaps UK	ITV1	19.6	1804
World Cup 2002: England vs. Denmark	Sport: Football	BBC1	18.9	1738
World Cup 2002: England vs. Nigeria	Sport: Football	BBC2	18.8	1733
World Cup 2002: England vs. Sweden	Sport: Football	ITV1	18.4	1696

Top children's programmes, 2002

All children Programme	Genre	Channel	Viewers %	Viewers 000's	Multichannel children Programme	Genre	Channel	Viewers %	Viewers 000's
Newsround	Factual	BBC1	10.9	1007	*All About Me*	Light Ent.	BBC1	7.8	446
Smart on the road	Factual	BBC1	10.7	989	*Newsround*	Factual	BBC1	6.7	385
All About Me Christmas at Club Blue Peter	Light Ent.	BBC1	10.6	976	*Bob the Builder*	Cartoons	BBC1	6.2	355
			10.4	958	*Stig of the Dump*	Drama	BBC1	6.1	352
CBBC at the Fame Academy	Light Ent.	BBC1	10.3	949	*Fingertips*	Factual	ITV1	6.1	349
					Smart on the Road	Factual	BBC1	6.1	348
Blue Peter	Factual	BBC1	9.9	915	*Blue Peter*	Factual	BBC1	6.0	346
Grange Hill	Drama	BBC1	9.7	894	*The Ghost Hunter*	Drama	BBC1	6.0	343
Film: *Snow White*	Cartoons	CH4	9.7	893	*The Cramp Twins*	Cartoons	BBC1	5.9	340
Viva S Club	Drama	BBC1	9.6	885	*The Story of Tracy Beaker*	Drama	BBC1	5.7	330
Mona the Vampire	Cartoons	BBC1	9.4	865					

Source: Broadcasting Standards Commission/Independent Television Commission

was carried out by Rosenblatt Research. The research included children's group discussions, mini groups and family observations in London, Birmingham, Manchester and Edinburgh and included those who had access to multichannel television or just the five terrestrial channels.

The report also highlights the current trends and the changes seen in the provision of children's television in the five years from, and including, 1996 (the period of time since the previous report) to 2001. The analysis is based on genre classifications defined by BARB for children's programmes. The advantage of using universally recognised industry data such as BARB is that it facilitates any future comparisons of trends. The genre categories used are: Children's Drama; Children's Factual; Children's Animation; Children's Light Entertainment and Children's Pre-school.

2. It should be noted that the BARB genre classifications for children's programming are not a complete reflection of programmes that are attractive to children. For example, certain US-originated comedy shows would be classified as 'Light Entertainment – Sitcom US' rather than 'Children's Light Entertainment'. By including 'Light Entertainment – Sitcom US' in the analysis, the figures would be distorted by the inclusion of those programmes within the genre which are not specifically targeted at children. This means that a number of programmes targeted at and of appeal to younger viewers may be excluded from this study. Similarly there are no data on the origin of production of the programmes, nor any detailed analysis of sub-categories within the genres. So 'animation' includes all manner of animation regardless of type or country of origin.

3. *What Children Watch* is the first piece in a series of research publications in which the BSC and ITC will be looking at issues relating to children's programming.

© Broadcasting Standards Commission/ Independent Television Commission

Bleak television landscape

TV regulator warns of too many soaps and not enough drama.
By Tom Leonard, Media Editor

Broadcasting regulators were warned yesterday that they risk creating a bleak television landscape of 'stripped down' budgets and 'commodity scheduling' of soaps and entertainment shows if they worry too much about economics rather than quality.

Patricia Hodgson, the chief executive of the outgoing Independent Television Commission, indicated that its successor, Ofcom, may become too caught up in competition and takeover issues rather than in the philosophy of public service broadcasting.

Regulators needed to be alert to the dangers of allowing financially straitened broadcasters to neglect expensive documentaries and dramas in favour of crowd-pleasing soaps and entertainment, she said.

In its final annual report, the ITC was most critical of ITV, whose viewing figures plummeted last year during the worst advertising recession in its history.

The commission claimed that soaps had reached saturation point on ITV, with five weekly instalments of *Coronation Street* and five of *Emmerdale*, creating a 'threat to diversity' in the channel's peak-time schedules between 6pm and 10.30pm.

The ITC also highlighted ITV's over-reliance on 'soft' celebrity-driven news and current affairs. The regulator noted that ITV was capable of producing high quality adaptations such as *The Forsyte Saga* and *Dr Zhivago* but had frequently held these back to show later in the evening when advertising revenue had picked up.

After an extra £100 million in funding for ITV, the ITC noted that the range and quality of its output had strengthened so far this year, especially in drama.

Viewers' organisations have complained that too much emphasis has been placed in the Communications Bill on pleasing broadcasters rather than audiences.

Ms Hodgson said Ofcom would need to understand not only the big economic issues affecting the television industry but also the micro-economics of how investment in programming could affect the quality of public service broadcasting.

'Economics is absolutely key, but it's not the only issue,' she said.

Despite Channel 4's pledge to rediscover its roots in making challenging television, the ITC indicated that it had relied too much on celebrity and leisure-based programmes. The report praised Channel 4's documentary output but criticised the 'disappointing' amount of contemporary drama.

Five was praised for improving its documentaries, reducing its reliance on crime and adult material and its 'adventurous' scheduling of peak-time arts programmes.

The ITC said there was a decline in religious programmes across all commercial channels.

© Telegraph Group Limited, London 2003

Getting into a lather

Family life in Britain's soaps

Many parents find soap operas can help them to discuss difficult issues with their children, and can help young people understand about family life, according to new research released to mark Parents' Week.

But while they accept that soaps are primarily for entertainment, some parents are concerned that the popular drama series broadcast material that is unsuitable for children, and would be better shown at a later hour.

For the report *Soaps and the Family*, released to highlight the third national Parents' Week, which runs from 21 to 27 October, the National Family and Parenting Institute (NFPI) put four of the nation's most popular drama series under the spotlight.

Over a month, family life as portrayed in *The Archers, Brookside, Coronation Street,* and *EastEnders* was analysed in depth. The findings show that while the soaps bring up major issues that affect parents and children, the way they portray families bears little relation to real life in Britain.

The soaps research was carried out to mark Parents' Week 2002, the third national awareness week for parents and children which aims to put families in the news, get parents' views heard, and celebrate the value and importance of being a parent. *Soaps and the Family* was commissioned to tie in with this year's Parents' Week theme, Images of Families, which aims to highlight the enormous importance of the media in family life today.

Chief executive of the NFPI, Mary MacLeod, said, 'Parents do not bring up their children in isolation, and the media has a huge effect on what they feel, believe and fear. Soaps are by far the most popular programmes on television – dramas about families watched by a family audience. This is the first time that British soaps have been looked at

from the perspective of the family and asking what the portrayal of family life is saying to parents and children.'

The majority of the parents surveyed in depth for the research said that they did discuss soap stories with their families, and that soaps were helpful in bringing up issues for discussion. Two-thirds believed that soap storylines could help children and young people to understand about family life, and 60 per cent that soaps could show how families can support each other. Parents were evenly divided on the question of when the soaps should be broadcast: 53 per cent believed current timings were suitable, whereas 46 per cent believed they should be broadcast later.

Key findings from the research include:
- *Coronation Street* had the most highly stereotyped characters, but also showed the most positive relationships between fathers and children
- *Brookside* featured the most effective family support, and the most family crises
- While there was little conflict in *The Archers, EastEnders* featured

scenes of serious conflict throughout, which frequently erupted into physical violence
- Children are usually in the background (sometimes disappearing altogether) and are often referred to as burdens or worries rather than as rewarding
- Men were portrayed as more sensible and level-headed than women
- Mothers tended to be shown as authoritarian
- There are many more single-parent families in the three television soaps than in real life – but fewer in *The Archers*
- Forty per cent of the families in *EastEnders*, 50 per cent in *Coronation Street* and 57 per cent in *Brookside* were intact two-parent families. *The Archers* had 89 per cent – the actual figure for the UK population is 74 per cent
- *Coronation Street* contains the highest proportion of broken families and also the highest number of single people
- While characters from ethnic minorities were featured, no programme attempted to give a sense of cultural diversity
- People with disabilities were

under-represented in all programmes, as were gay men. Lesbian women and bisexual people were not portrayed at all

The researchers also highlighted a number of scenes and stories that underlined a sense of unreality in the programmes. For example, three disappearing under-fives in an animal enclosure during *Brookside*; and the immediate recovery of Janine Butcher in *EastEnders* from agoraphobia. Also mentioned were the 'bad fairies' who seemed to emerge every time it seemed that a happy ending might be achieved by soap characters.

Questioned on the suitability of topics included in soaps, most parents believed that issues such as terminal and mental illness, AIDS, teenage pregnancy and infidelity were acceptable. Three out of four parents

(75 per cent) believed that domestic violence and suicide were acceptable, but the use of firearms (67 per cent), rape (65 per cent) and incest (58 per cent) were acceptable to fewer parents.

Eighty per cent of the parents believed that soaps did not promote positive images of the family, highlighting too many scenes of sex and violence, a high level of infidelity, alcohol abuse and an

overall feeling of negativity as areas of concern. At the same time, they accepted that soaps were made to entertain, and that dramatic story-lines – however improbable – were needed to attract viewers.

Soaps and the Family includes in-depth analysis of the family life portrayed in each of the four dramas, in particular the way in which parents interact with their children and how conflict is dealt with in soap families.

■ More than 100 parents were surveyed, including a majority from the NFPI's Parents' Panel, plus others who contacted the NFPI via their website poll on soaps on www.nfpi.org

■ The above information is from NFPI's web site which can be found at www.nfpi.org

Gun culture on TV

Information from mediawatch-uk

In a letter from the Home Office to mediawatch-uk the Government says 'it is important that the media promotes positive and responsible images'.

John Beyer, Director of mediawatch-uk, said that he believed the media should not exclude itself from the multi-agency approach to tackling gun culture. 'For far too long the entertainment industry has denied its responsibility for influencing the state of our society. It is no longer a credible or rational position to suggest that the media simply reflects society as it is. Increasingly, society reflects the worst excesses of the media. In line with the firearms amnesty announced yesterday by the Home Secretary there needs to be an amnesty with regard to firearms in TV drama and film,' he said.

In a new report, *Promoting a Culture of Violence 2*, analysing 183 films shown on the five terrestrial TV channels in 2002, mediawatch-uk has identified 966 incidents involving firearms, 701 violent

assaults and 223 incidents involving knives and other offensive weapons. Channel 5 TV is again found to be the worst offender because of the high proportion, 33%, of all films shown on the terrestrial channels.

Mr Beyer said: 'We are delighted that the Home Office recognises the importance of promoting positive

and responsible images and we welcome Dr Kim Howells' recent criticism of violence in entertainment. We also welcome the review of Britain's censorship laws announced last month by Lord Warner. The findings of our report again show that the broadcasting industry shamelessly continues to promote a culture of violence and pays no attention to the damaging influence on our society.'

Mr Beyer concluded: 'We hope that OFCOM, in drawing up its more coherent system of objectives and principles, will embrace a much broader definition of incitement as set out in Clause 307 of the Communications Bill. The continual portrayal of violence on television should itself be regarded as an incitement to crime and disorder. We urge the House of Lords to amend the Bill in the weeks ahead.'

■ The above information is from mediawatch-uk's web site which can be found at www.mediawatchuk.org

BBC *to provide more warnings of adult content*

By Patrick Barrett

The BBC director of television Jana Bennett has admitted she has serious concerns about some of the television content children are exposed to.

Indicating the BBC was preparing to provide greater guidance to viewers about sex and violence in programmes, she said parents were right to be worried about TV content.

'It is hard to make assumptions about what children are aware of,' Ms Bennett said.

'I recently had to steer my eight-year-old away from a music channel showing the pop duo Tatu kissing, kissing and kissing some more.

'My eight-year-old informed me they were kissing because they were lesbians. I didn't even know she knew the word.'

Explaining why the BBC chose not to broadcast Tatu's video but screened a gay kiss on *Casualty* last week, Ms Bennett said the BBC had a duty to make parents feel safe and should not court controversy for the sake of it.

'*Top of the Pops* is an early evening programme watched by children. The latter was a legitimate part of a drama for a mixed audience. Neither decision was taken lightly,' she said.

Speaking at a seminar on the impact of TV on the family, organised by the Broadcasting Standards Commission and the National Family and Parenting Institute, Ms Bennett said the BBC would reinforce the 9pm watershed with more warnings about content.

> '**It is hard to make assumptions about what children are aware of, I recently had to steer my eight-year-old away from a music channel showing the pop duo Tatu kissing, kissing and kissing some more**'

'The watershed is still a structural guide that is valuable. It creates a point in the evening where parents and broadcasters must exercise care,' she said.

'But I think we all recognise the watershed is not the only signpost we should use. We will take care to provide verbal warnings.'

John Yorke, the BBC head of drama who was poached by Channel 4 this week, rejected suggestions that producers were driven by ratings rather than responsibility to their viewers.

He said soaps such as *EastEnders* and *Brookside* were fundamentally moral and the issue of morality had been raised in every meeting he had attended to discuss *EastEnders* storylines.

'We have found that more people watch it if that happens,' Mr Yorke said.

'We live in a dark world. *EastEnders* has always gone into it with a very responsible and mature approach and never cynically exploited issues for the sake of ratings.'

Mr Yorke said he took issue with the BSC's censure of *EastEnders* for its depiction of 'Trevor shoving little Mo's head in a tray of gravy'.

'As far as we know no one went out and beat up their wife after it but we know a number of women did leave their husbands,' he said.

© *Guardian Newspapers Limited 2003*

A brand new kind of advert

Kids are king and schoolyards the new marketplace, writes Simon Caulkin

Here are some frightening statistics: a three-year-old child can recognise brand logos and brand loyalty can be influenced from the age of two; the average British, Australian or American child will be exposed to 20,000-40,000 ads a year; American children spend 60 per cent more time in front of the TV screen each year than they do at school.

In the US, four- to 12-year-olds spent about £35 billion in 2001, but influenced 60 per cent of their parents' brand purchases – overall, their total global purchasing influence adds up to an unimaginable $188 trillion.

Such figures trip relentlessly from the tongue of Martin Lindstrom, the hyperactive main author of *Brandchild* (Kogan Page), a new book that claims to be the first to chart the relationship of children to brands.

Lindstrom – himself looking disconcertingly young – says that although the world he is portraying has a hallucinatory quality in some respects, it is not fanciful – being based on a year-long survey of 2,000 'tweenagers' (eight to 14) across 15 countries by market researcher Millward Brown.

Tweens are so technologically attuned that technology itself is of no interest except when it goes wrong. Forty per cent think, almost certainly rightly, they know more about computers than their parents; 10 per cent have their own website (and 50 per cent want one). They're deeply interested in brands, in fact they define themselves through and against them, but partly because of the technology tweens' relationship to brands is quite different from that of their parents.

'We were brought up on passive media, but a whole new generation is completely interactive,' says Lindstrom, who believes that so far the ad industry has miserably failed to respond to the implications. 'Interactivity is as big as TV.'

Equipment in eldest child's bedroom

Homes with children tend to have a wider range of new technologies in the home. Two-thirds (59%) of people with children have access to multichannel television, while only 46% without children have it.

	Total	0-3	Age of children 4-9	10-15
Television	57%	33%	58%	79%
Radio	48%	21%	49%	69%
Games console	28%	16%	27%	42%
Video cassette recorder	32%	18%	31%	46%
Computer	12%	2%	12%	19%
Satellite/cable	6%	1%	4%	11%
Computer with internet	3%	2%	4%	5%

Source: The Public's View 2002, Independent Television Commission and Broadcasting Standards Commission, 2003

In keeping with the interactive relationship, the tween generation is radically more demanding of brands than their parents. Schoolyards are 'brand showrooms', but tweens want brands to be available 24/7, and to dialogue with them, as a matter of course. Brands take the place of religion in a godless world, but paradoxically that makes individual brands more vulnerable, not less.

In the US, four- to 12-year-olds spent about £35 billion in 2001, but influenced 60 per cent of their parents' brand purchases

---

Loyalties are strong, but the need for instant gratification also means that they can be dropped without a second thought. 'You're 100 per cent interactive – or dead,' says Lindstrom. 'That's where you hit the wall. You can't build a brand on frustration.'

Many big mass brands as we currently know them are doomed – dim-witted survivors from the pre-interactive age, unable to enter the restless, emotional, fantasy-driven world of the pre-teens, concludes Lindstrom. In some respects these proto-consumers are deeply fearful and conservative. They identify completely with the family and are constantly looking for meaning.

In other respects, however, they are old beyond their years. They are well on the way, for instance, to developing their own global language of brands. Thirty per cent of tweens communicate internationally, according to the survey. 'I've seen it with my own eyes,' says Lindstrom. 'Grammar is disappearing – this is the first generation which is creating its own global language with icons and mobile phones.'

At the same time, the information overload that paralysed older generations no longer has any meaning for kids who have grown up in it: like a fish in water, that's the environment they live in. As a result, they have 'X-ray eyes', able to spot and discard in a microsecond anything in the brand that smacks of the phoney, the false, the me-too, the pompous and the bland – conventional advertising, in fact.

Lindstrom thinks the implications for companies are daunting. How can they construct a brand that appeals to both the impatient young and their parents? A brand that's cool, honest, has attitude, is interactive? The answer is, they can't. 'The cool ones are the anti-brands,' believes Lindstrom, who predicts that underneath a global umbrella brand, companies will divide their lines into 100s, even 1,000s of individual brands.

At the extreme, kids will become brands themselves (remember the website statistics), with their own merchandising plans. Already some companies are experimenting with sponsoring individual tweens – in surfing, skateboarding or whatever, some as young as eight or nine – in return for promotion of their brand. Pepsi is signing up children to join an advisory group. 'Fifteen years from now, kids will be putting value in the brand bank, not just salary. They'll be their own brand platform. Big companies will have to accommodate their attitudes and flavour to that.'

In this emerging world, kids don't play with conventional toys any more – there's no time, because they're consuming media: watching TV or DVDs, texting or playing computer games.

This has depressing effects on children's creativity, but it's a trend that's hard to stop. Product placement, positive but also sometimes negative, is the new advertising.

'The motion picture, whether on TV or in the cinema, has become the lifeblood of tween brands.'

Lindstrom is scathing of the ad industry's slowness to move beyond the traditional offering of two-dimensional advertising. To communicate immediately and engagingly with the new generation, he says, it will have to learn to fuse all the senses into the brand message: sound, sight, touch, smell, taste. Some companies use one or other of these – the smell of bread in supermarkets, the snap, crackle and pop of breakfast cereals – but brand-building needs to appeal to all of them, according to Lindstrom. A brand can't take a breather; there's no place for companies to hide.

'Sound + sight + smell + taste + touch = brand', says Lindstrom. It may not be a world you like, he says: but as you can't escape it, the best chance of influencing it is to run towards it at full speed.

■ This article first appeared in *The Observer*, 6 April 2003.

© *Guardian Newspapers Limited 2003*

Children and advertising

The effect of advertising on children and the use of children in advertisements are sensitive issues. The British Code of Advertising, Sales Promotion and Direct Marketing (the CAP Code) – the self-regulatory guidelines written by the advertising industry – include vital requirements in this area

The rules

When dealing with complaints about advertisements featuring or aimed at children, the ASA is guided by the following basic principle:

Advertisements 'addressed to, targeted at or featuring children should contain nothing which is likely to result in their physical, mental or moral harm, or to exploit their credulity, loyalty, vulnerability or lack of experience'.

Advertising aimed at children

Today's consumer receives hundreds of advertising messages each day. Adults can view these with a sceptical eye, but children are more vulnerable. The CAP Code contains special rules for advertisers who target this group:

ASA

Pester power

A crucial requirement of the CAP Code is that advertisements targeting children should not actively encourage them to make a nuisance of themselves to parents or others. One magazine advertisement for a children's TV channel was criticised by the ASA for suggesting that children without access to it should complain to their parents.

Easy to understand

Advertisers should not exaggerate the appeal or performance of a product. A toy, for instance, must not be shown to be larger than it really is. Complex issues should not be over-simplified: in 2001 complaints were upheld about leaflets sent out by a pressure group that encouraged children to stop drinking milk by implying that milk consumption caused acne, obesity, flatulence and excess phlegm.

Direct appeals

Goods which are considered too expensive for the majority of children to buy should not be advertised to children. An electronics firm advertising computer software at prices starting from £40 in a children's

publication was criticised by the ASA; most children would not be able to afford them.

Popularity

Advertisements should not make children feel inferior or unpopular for not buying the advertised product. The ASA upheld a complaint against an advertisement that showed a grinning boy being scowled at enviously by two other boys, whose faces had been shaded green. The headline ran: 'Who's Got The New [Computer] then?'

Responsible

Advertisements should not encourage children to eat or drink at or near bedtime, to eat frequently throughout the day or to replace main meals with sweets and snacks.

Parental permission

Advertisements should make clear to children that they must obtain permission to buy complex or expensive products. For sales

> *Today's consumer receives hundreds of advertising messages each day. Adults can view these with a sceptical eye, but children are more vulnerable*

promotions where the prizes may cause a conflict between parent and child, consent is also required.

Advertising which features children

The safety of children is of paramount importance in advertisements and they must not, either by message or example, lead a child into a potentially dangerous situation. The Code details a number of specific requirements in this area. The general rule is that: 'Children should not be encouraged to copy any practice that might be unsafe for a child.'

Advertisements should not encourage children to talk to strangers or enter strange places. Children should not be depicted unattended in street scenes or shown playing in the road unless they are old enough to be responsible for their own safety. Likewise, they should always be seen to observe the Highway Code. Children should not be shown using or in close proximity to dangerous substances such as medicines or equipment such as electrical appliances, without direct adult supervision.

The advertiser responsible for a poster, which featured two boys, one of whom was taking out a gun from inside his jacket was asked to withdraw the advertisement. The ASA also upheld a complaint concerning a poster for a fruit drink that showed a young boy drinking from a bottle whilst swimming underwater because it considered that the poster irresponsibly portrayed an unsafe activity.

Subject, context and choice of media

Advertisers would break the CAP Code if the approach they used was violent or capable of disturbing young readers. In judging such complaints, the Authority takes into account the context in which the advertisement appeared and the relevance of the advertisers' approach.

> *In 2002, the ASA received 13,959 complaints, 1,531 which concerned advertising and children of which 25 of the ads were upheld*

Facts and figures

In 2002, the ASA received 13,959 complaints, 1,531 of which concerned advertising and children (relating to 139 ads). Of these, complaints about 25 of the ads were upheld. This compares with a total of 12,595 complaints received in 2001; 496 concerned advertising and children (relating to 63 ads – one ad generated 125 complaints alone) of which 170 (concerning 16 advertisements) were upheld.

■ The above information is from the Advertising Standards Authority's web site which can be found at www.asa.org.uk

© *Advertising Standards Authority (ASA)*

Serious offence in non-broadcast advertising

Executive summary. Information from the Advertising Standards Authority

- The ASA commissioned a quantitative study which examined the views of the UK population as a whole on the nature and causes of 'serious offence'.

- A representative sample of 2,082 adults aged 15+ in the United Kingdom were interviewed using a random location sampling technique. All interviews were conducted using Computer Aided Personal Interviewing (CAPI).

- The majority of the population are quite positive towards advertising, but some feel that sometimes ads just go too far. However, a similar proportion felt that some people are just too sensitive about the things they see in advertising.

- Just under a fifth of adults said that they had been personally offended by advertising they had seen in the past 12 months, and 'push' media such as posters and direct mail were most likely to cause personal offence. Internet advertising was the medium most likely to cause personal and serious offence among those who had seen it.

- Women, older people and those from non-white ethnic minorities, as well as those from higher social grades were more likely to have been personally offended in the past 12 months. Men were more likely to have been offended on behalf of others, as were young people.

- Issues related to children and advertising were seen as having the greatest potential to cause offence. Almost all respondents thought that the portrayal of children in a sexual way had the potential to cause serious offence, and similarly high proportions thought that showing images or words unsuitable for children to see or hear was also potentially offensive. As well as being concerned about the content of advertising aimed at children, the majority of the public were also concerned about children when thinking about the location and context of the advertising. There was very strong feeling that advertisers should take special care if children may see the ad or if the ad is shown in places where children go.

- The nature of serious offence differs between younger and older people, and young people tended to be less sensitive around 'traditionally' offensive areas such as sexual images, violence and bad language. Young people tended to be more sensitive than their older counterparts when thinking about the way in which people are portrayed, and they tend to be more concerned about the portrayal of vulnerable groups.

- The public acknowledged that niche targeting is possible when advertising in magazines, and felt that you should know what you are letting yourself in for when buying a particular publication. However, it was felt that there are certain publications which could be bought for general

Offence in advertising

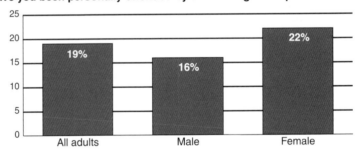

Have you been personally offended by advertising in the past 12 months?

All adults: 19%
Male: 16%
Female: 22%

Personal offence in the past 12 months within each advertising medium

The table below shows the proportions who have been personally offended by an advertisement in the past 12 months in each medium in the ASA's remit. It should be remembered that not all respondents would have seen advertising in each medium. To account for this the column on the right of the table shows the proportion of those respondents who have seen some advertising in each medium in the past 12 months who have been personally offended by advertising there.

Medium	% of all adults personally offended by ad	% of those seen medium in past 12 months personally offended
Posters or billboards	7	9
Direct mail	6	7
Newspapers	5	6
Magazines	5	6
Internet	5	12
Sales promotion	4	4
Cinema	2	3

Source: Serious Offence in Non-Broadcast Advertising, Advertising Standards Authority

consumption and one should be confident that these would not contain shocking advertising.

- The majority of the public thought that advertising could be more shocking if it is 'in a good cause', but there was less support for commercial advertising to deliver shocking messages.

- The majority of UK adults agreed that advertising which caused widespread and serious offence should be banned, and this feeling was strongly and widely held. There was less support for banning advertising where offence was not serious or widespread. Those who had themselves been offended by advertising in the past were more likely to feel that offensive advertising should be banned.

Conclusions

The nature of offence

- The reaction of offence can be broken down into 'emotional' offence and 'rational' offence:
  – We have suggested that 'emotional' offence can be equated with 'serious' offence.
- Individuals are far more likely to have been offended 'by proxy' (on behalf of somebody else) than to have been offended personally:
  – However, where the offence is 'by proxy' rather than 'personal' the reaction generally tends to be rational rather than emotional.

Issues causing offence

- There appeared to be a difference in the issues that provoked serious offence among younger and older people:
  – Younger people tended to be less sensitive in relation to 'traditionally' offensive areas, such as sexual images, violence and bad language;
  – But they tended to be more sensitive than older people when thinking about how groups and individuals were portrayed, and were more concerned about the negative portrayal of vulnerable groups.
  – Minority groups did seem to be far more sensitive than did the general population:
  – And there seemed to be differ-

ences in their views of the images that caused offence;
  – Issues that were very emotive and sensitive for minority ethnic and religious groups (such as religious symbols, perceived racism, sex and violence) tended to be viewed by the majority as being less important, in the context of other issues.

- However, there was consensus between the minority and majority groups that the images that were most sensitive were:
  – The portrayal of children, and particularly any sexualisation of children;
  – Images felt to degrade, demean or humiliate vulnerable groups.

Factors affecting offence

- It was clear that the reactions of both the overall population and minority groups were greatly affected by the context in which the advert appeared:
  – The location and type of media were crucial;
  – They influenced who would see the advert, with particular concern expressed as to whether children would see it and whether groups likely to be offended (such as religious groups) would see it;
  – As well as determining how much choice individuals felt that they had as to whether they viewed an advert or not;
  – And whether individuals were likely to see the advert in company with others.

- Additionally, the likelihood of an advert causing offence was affected by the presence of humour in the advert and by the origin of the advert:
  – Adverts produced by charities or Government were felt to be able to use shocking or distressing

images to a far greater extent without offending than were commercial organisations.

Quantitative research objectives and method

The quantitative research aimed to assess the following:

- What proportion of the public have recently been offended by non-broadcast advertising they have seen, and how serious was this offence
- What is the influence of context in terms of serious offence. This could include the timing of the ad, the medium in which the ad appears and the nature of the advertiser
- General attitudes towards non-broadcast advertising in the UK.

Quantitative research method

Given the objectives described above, a face-to-face in-home interview was judged to be the most appropriate method. For reasons of cost efficiency, questions were placed on BMRB's face-to-face omnibus, and the first phase of fieldwork was conducted between 13 and 19 December 2001. Interviews were conducted among a representative sample of 2,082 adults aged 15+ in the United Kingdom using a random location sampling technique. All interviews were conducted using Computer Assisted Personal Interviewing (CAPI). After the end of the first tranche of fieldwork, it was decided that one issue required clarification which was attitudes to government and charity vs commercial advertising. A small second tranche of fieldwork was completed between 28 February and 6 March 2002. At this stage 989 adults in Great Britain were interviewed, again face to face in-home. Because this questionnaire was very small, it was not appropriate to run a separate survey in Northern Ireland, so results for these questions are among adults in Great Britain only.

- The above information is from a Summary Research Report: *Serious Offence in Non-Broadcast Advertising*, by the Advertising Standards Authority, July 2002. The report was prepared by BMRB Social Research.
© *Advertising Standards Authority (ASA)*

Cracking the Communications Bill

If you're studying British broadcasting since the 1990s – or any other aspect of broadcasting, in fact – you'll probably have to get to grips with the ongoing debates about the new Communications Bill, which will have a huge impact on the structure, ownership and output of the broadcast media in the UK. Introduced in May 2002, the Bill is unlikely to become law until November 2003 at the earliest; but the amendments, lobbying and arguments about it will run and run. Here, with the help of Broadcast Magazine *and a trawl of the archives at* **www.guardianunlimited.co.uk**, *we attempt to unpick the issues that will really matter.*

Key proposals of the draft Communications Bill – and what they mean

About cross-media ownership

- Non-European companies, including Australian or American firms, can now own UK TV channels.

  This means that companies such as Disney or AOL Time Warner can buy into Britain's most popular TV channel, ITV.

  Granada, which has shown an interest in becoming the sole owner of ITV by merging with its main rival, Carlton, could be thwarted by this clause. Carlton has strong American connections, which it could sell out to, rather than merging with Granada. News International mogul Rupert Murdoch, however, would be barred from owning ITV because of the rule below …

- Newspaper groups can own TV channels. But those with more than 20% of the newspaper market cannot own more than 20% of an ITV service.

  This clause should ensure that commercial TV cannot be controlled by big Press barons. It does not, however, apply to Channel 5 (see below) – probably much to Rupert Murdoch's relief.

- A single company can own both a national TV channel and a national radio station.

- Local commercial radio companies can merge; the existing rule which limits the number of stations owned by any single operator is to be scrapped. Newspaper groups are also now able to own radio stations.

  For example, the owners of the *Daily Mail*, *Metro* and the *Evening Standard*, Associated Newspapers, could bid to take over Capital Radio.

- No company which dominates local presses will be allowed to own the regional TV licence in the same area.

  In theory this will protect regional audiences from powerful local cross-media interests and ensure diversity of news coverage.

- At least three commercial voices in addition to the BBC must exist in newspapers, television and radio in local communities.

  This restriction should prevent any monopolisation in local media output.

- ITV may be owned by a single owner.

- A single company can own both an ITV licence and Channel 5.

  Channel 5 looks set to become a major focus of ownership battles. Despite its weedy 6% share of the audience, it's less regulated than other commercial broadcasters, and has no obligations to provide a

regional programme – and its audience and profile are growing.

- C5 is currently 65% owned by RTL, the biggest terrestrial broadcaster in Europe, and backed by huge German media group Bertelsmann, which also wants to get its hands on UK TV. If it bought C5, it would have its way in.
- If Rupert Murdoch bought C5 into his empire – something he's wanted to do for a long time – it would be aggressively marketed through his papers and Sky (which already broadcasts its *Sunrise* news show on C5), and its market share would probably overtake ITV. Murdoch's power would then be virtually unstoppable.
- BSkyB has been extremely interested in Channel 5, but spokespersons say it has 'no immediate plans' to buy.
- Newspaper groups can buy Channel 5.

About regulation and Ofcom

Ofcom: The Office of Communications – the new super-regulator which is made up of, and oversees, the Broadcasting Standards Commission, the Independent Television Commission, the Radio Authority, the Radio Communications Agency, and Oftel, the Office of Telecommunications. Interestingly, it will not incorporate the British Board of Film Classification (BBFC).

- Ofcom must review the rules about media ownership every three years.
- Ofcom must be run by a board which includes all nations of the UK, plus a consumers' panel.
- Ofcom has the power to investigate news and current affairs programming of any local radio service.
- If the ownership of a company changes, Ofcom will have the power to vary its licence to ensure that the 'character' of the service is maintained. But Ofcom may only intervene if licensed broadcasters fail to deliver what they promised.
- Ofcom will oversee, extend, or revoke a nominated news provider (i.e. a news provider

approved by the ITC arm of Ofcom) for ITV and Channel 5. No single company can own more than 40% of the chosen provider.

This means that Independent Television News (ITN) can never be completely controlled by any single ITV company – an acknowledgement of the public's need for 'independent' news – and that there is quality control of the news coverage.

- Holders of ITV licences must provide adequate financial support for their news provider.

A way of ensuring that ITN's resources are not squeezed too tight – last year its contract to ITV was cut by £10m, amid public concern about the quality of news coverage.

- Three levels of regulation are to be introduced, including more self-regulation by broadcasters.

Ofcom will ensure that:

- basic taste and decency, independent production quotas and equal opportunities standards are met
- each of the terrestrial channels provides an annual statement about its public service responsibilities, which Ofcom will supervise and monitor
- there is a consumers' panel representing the voice of the public.

It will be able to impose fines if its standards are not met.

- Ofcom is to regulate the basic standards of the BBC, but the BBC governors will still supervise the quality of its output.

No change there then; the BBC will still be able to exert its own quality control – which unsurprisingly other broadcasters aren't too pleased about . . . MPs claim that this creates 'an unlevel playing field to everyone's disadvantage'; why should the BBC

be allowed to monitor itself? On the other hand, the BBC will be subject to the same fines as other channels (up to £250,000) if it fails to meet its standards.

- Broadcasters will still be required to commission 25% of their output from independent producers.

The Bill claims that this 25% quota has 'helped maintain the diversity of British television, supported the development of creative and technical skills, and helped create a thriving and innovative production industry'.

- Telecommunications systems will no longer require a licence; they merely have to conform to a set of standards, such as offering 999 calls.

Since BT was privatised in the early 1980s, telecoms firms have had to apply for licenses – there are currently nearly 400 of them. This new clause could release BT from controls which have kept its prices down for the last 10 years. But it seems likely that there will be increased competition, and as a result, the cost of a phone call will continue to fall in price. Over the last 18 years, phone bills have halved in real terms.

However, BT will have stricter quality control – good news for some.

- Companies can buy spectrum (broadcasting airwave space) from an existing user.

Currently unlicensed TV companies such as satellite operators do not pay for the airwaves they transmit on. Channels such as BSkyB may now have to pay for guaranteed access to the spectrum.

- Consultation on the Bill closes on 2nd August.

So there it is: the new Broadcasting Bill in all its glory. Things will of course change – and may already have done so by the time you read this. If you're interested in how laws get made, how interest groups like regulators can lobby for changes, and how broadcasting policies such as this can shape your viewing, watch this space.

For the last word, here are some soundbite responses from the broadcasters, critics and regulators themselves:

'For too long the UK's media have been over-regulated and over-protected from competition. The draft bill . . . will liberalise the market, so removing unnecessary regulatory burdens and cutting red tape, but at the same time retain some key safeguards that will protect the diversity and plurality of our media.'

Tessa Jowell,
Secretary of State for Media

'There are some disturbing themes . . . the danger of various kinds of dominance in the purchase of TV rights, if a single player dominates pay TV and terrestrial TV . . . this danger seems to be growing . . . I believe deregulation could boost quality and diversity. But we have to be sure that diversity does not become its opposite.'

Mark Thomas,
Chief Executive of Channel 4

'My real concern is with the scrapping of the rules preventing non-European ownership. This will really give the global media groups – mainly but not exclusively US-based – the green light to move into UK broadcasting. UK media groups are minnows and will be easy prey to these huge predators . . . As powerful commercial media bulk out and fill more of our channels, what future for public service broadcasting in 10 years' time?'

Granville Williams,
Campaign for Press and
Broadcasting Freedom

'This is not about news coverage but about who is controlling access to our most influential channels of communication, whether it be in drama, comedy, children's programmes, sport, documentaries or the arts. It's not about political bias but about encouraging multiple voices and different frames of reference. It's about alternative ways of looking at the world which are not derived from the corporate philosophy of News International.

Within five years, one organisation and one individual could be controlling over a third of our national press and our most popular free-to-air channel, as well as dictating terms of access to the dominant digital TV platform.'

Steven Barnett, *Observer*
broadcasting columnist,
Professor of Communications,
University of Westminster

'There is much to praise, but it remains strikingly unimaginative when it talks about the economics of production in the UK ... There seems little hope of securing genuine competition when the BBC is still given room to wriggle out of Ofcom's grasp.'

John McVay, Chief Executive of Pact, the Producers' Alliance for Cinema and Television – the trade association for independent producers of TV, film, animation and new technologies. It represents over 1000 independent production companies.
■ The above information is from *MediaMagazine*, produced by the English and Media Centre. See page 41 for their address details.

© English and Media Centre

Why the Communications Bill is bad news

The Communications Bill – what's at stake?

'For too long the UK's media have been over-regulated and over-protected from competition . . . The draft Bill we published today will liberalise the market, so removing unnecessary regulatory burdens and cutting red tape.'

This was how Tessa Jowell, Secretary of State for the Department of Culture, Media and Sport, announced the publication of the draft Communications Bill on May 7th 2002. Her words left not the slightest doubt about the Bill's underlying assumption – the drive to less regulation in the media.

While asserting that the Communications Bill will protect 'diversity and plurality in the media', Tessa Jowell praised its main proposals using terms drawn straight from the big business phrase book. In signalling that the Bill was intended to

By Tom O'Malley

'liberalise' communications, by cutting 'red tape' she all too clearly indicated the Government's willingness to construct a communications system run primarily on market principles.

But does this really matter?

If you woke up to learn that the Government planned to 'liberalise' education or health and promote

We have seen what liberalisation has done to the railways in the UK

market forces, you would know exactly what it meant. You would expect the further undermining of public service values in these areas and the replacement of such values by the principle of 'those who have the most money get the best health or education service'.

We have seen what liberalisation has done to the railways in the UK. The language used by the Secretary of State means that a similar fate awaits the public service broadcasters – in other words, all of television and radio in the UK except services provided exclusively by cable and satellite operators.

We cannot do without a strong public service media system in the UK. For all its faults, it provides the whole population, not just those who can afford the costly fees for pay-TV, with access to a world of information, education and entertainment, at extremely low cost. Without a public service system broad enough to reflect the lives and concerns of a wide cross-section of the community, the quality of our cultural and democratic life would be much, much poorer.

In the USA where global media corporations milk the media for profits, the provision of news, current affairs and high quality programming is marginal – and the US democratic system suffers as a result. Commenting on the USA, Robert McChesney has pointed out that: 'the poor have all but disappeared from the media. And in those rare cases where poor people are covered, studies show that the news media reinforce racist stereotypes, playing into the social myopia of the middle and upper classes.'

McChesney and others stress the ways in which a heavily market-orientated communications system undermines popular culture and democracy by allowing commercial forces to wholly dominate the media.

The proposals in the draft Communications Bill seek to further open up the UK media to takeovers by global media conglomerates. These conglomerates are determined to keep costs low and profits high. They will increase the amount of cheap programming imports, thereby undermining levels of employment and skills in the media, as well as working conditions. In their ruthless, profit-driven world, editorial independence comes a poor second to profit maximisation.

Put bluntly, the forces unleashed by the proposals in the draft Communications Bill will massively commercialise the media in the UK producing a deeply negative effect on their objectivity, range and quality and undermining public service values.

Even the joint committee of MPs and peers set up under Lord Puttnam to scrutinise the Bill expressed its 'unease on several grounds' and included recommendations on how the Bill might be strengthened to safeguard media plurality and standards of public service broadcasting.

This article outlines some of the key proposals in the draft Communications Bill and their implications. It points to the kind of

action that needs to be taken by all of us to construct better legislation, defend our media as a public service and help to promote a more open and a richer democratic and cultural life in the UK.

The draft Bill – key proposals

Here we outline some of the key proposals in the draft Communications Bill and point to their implications.

The proposals in the draft Communications Bill seek to further open up the UK media to takeovers by global media conglomerates

---

OFCOM

The Government is setting up a new super-regulator called the Office of Communications (OFCOM). It will swallow up separate regulators like the Independent Television Commission, the Radio Authority, the Office of Telecommunications and the Broadcasting Standards Commission.

The Government says OFCOM is needed in order to rationalise communications regulations. But while OFCOM will have some powers over the BBC and S4C, the national and regional press – major players in the media industry – are left largely outside OFCOM.

OFCOM is designed 'to operate with a high degree of collective responsibility and concentrate on effectiveness and function rather than representation of particular interests'. This is why the Government has flatly refused requests to make its Board broader and more representative, by including nominated members from the English Regions and the devolved authorities.

The Government has constructed a Board which will have four part-time, non-executive members, none with the slightest semblance of a democratic mandate. The man selected to run OFCOM, Lord David Currie, Dean of the City University Business School, has no discernible experience of broadcasting or cultural policy.

OFCOM is designed 'to promote competition in the provision and making available of . . . services and facilities'. It has a clear obligation to ensure that regulation by OFCOM does not involve '(a) the imposition of burdens which are unnecessary; or (b) the maintenance of burdens which have become unnecessary'.

The framework created by the Government is therefore designed to encourage the progressive removal of obligations (which it reinterprets as 'burdens') on broadcasters. These obligations, as sure as night follows day, will be described as 'unnecessary' by commercial radio and TV operators facing fierce competition in a freshly deregulated market place.

The fact that OFCOM is intended to emphasise economic issues rather than promote high quality content is illustrated by the status given to the two bodies within the organisation charged with looking after content and consumer issues. The Content Board and the Consumer Panel are unequal, with the latter having much greater power to influence OFCOM, and much greater independence, than the former.

OFCOM will have the job of dealing with complaints from the public about the media. Thus the licenser and regulator is also the investigator, judge and jury on questions of complaints.

Public service broadcasting

Public service provisions, in the full sense, are relegated to the BBC, Channel 4 and S4C and, to lesser extents, ITV and C5. The policing of the key public service requirements will be carried out largely by self-regulation, a method that has failed miserably in the national newspaper industry. The system proposed is largely one of 'negative' and quota-driven regulation.

Tier 1 will provide a list of 'don'ts' for broadcasters. Tier 2 has a list of 'quotas' for independent, regional and educational productions, and for news and current affairs programmes. The temptation here will be for companies to fulfil their quota requirements with poor quality, cheaply produced programmes. Tier 3, the policing of high level public service requirements, which in the new system are largely the responsibility of BBC, C4 and S4C, is left to self-regulation.

The underlying idea here is to set up transitional arrangements to allow, in the future, for OFCOM to have the bare minimum role in promoting high quality broadcast content.

The Communications Bill contains no major safeguards for the continuation of significant local or regional production centres outside of the London area. In the future neither the BBC nor commercial companies will have to run production centres in places like Cardiff or Manchester. The Bill only requires

OFCOM to ensure that companies 'include what appears to OFCOM to be an appropriate range and proportion of programmes made outside the M25 area' but this could mean Reading as much as Wales or Scotland.

The BBC and OFCOM

The Government plans that the BBC will be 'subject to increased external regulation while other public service broadcasters will face reduced external regulation. Thus the BBC's position will be brought closer to other broadcasters'.

Thus OFCOM, whose main purpose is to promote economic competition in the media as well as to lift 'burdens' in the sector, will be bringing its overwhelmingly commercially orientated outlook to bear on scrutinising the BBC. OFCOM will supervise the BBC's programming codes, production quotas, the amount of its original productions and the range and timing of news.

The effect of this will be to create a situation where the commercial operators, whose interests OFCOM has been created to uphold, are able to pressurise OFCOM into demanding that the BBC does not compete with them in areas where the commercial operators believe they could make a killing.

Thus the BBC's remit in areas such as popular comedy, sport and drama will come under direct pressure from the commercial sector. The commercial companies will want the BBC to leave this type of programming to them. Similarly any plans the BBC might have for expanding public services could be threatened.

Ownership

The Communications Bill is designed to 'simplify and liberalise the rules on media ownership'. It abolishes rules restricting ownership

of the UK media to nationals of the European Economic Area (EEA). This opens the door to US ownership of the UK media, while US law strongly protects its media from UK takeover.

Following through the Government's plans to 'reduce cross-media regulation' the Communications Bill will also make it easier for newspapers to merge and for ITV to be dominated by one company.

The result will be intensified cross-media ownership and concentration. The bigger the newly 'liberated' media companies, the more they will seek to maximise profits by standardising their content. This will lead to pressures on the ITV and commercial radio companies to ditch local content, local and regional coverage, and substitute it with cheap, easily produced material. And since it is OFCOM's express purpose to promote competition and cut 'red tape' it is likely to be inclined to act in the interests of promoting commercial efficiency.

In addition the Government plans to allow advertising agencies and religious groups to own TV stations. Advertising agencies are global conglomerates with interests in all aspects of the commercial media. Allowing them to own TV stations will simply extend their power to undermine the quality and objectivity of programming in the interests of profit. If religious TV in the USA is a guide, granting ownership rights to TV in the UK to religious groups is likely to lead to the growth of highly conservative religious stations.

Note

Thanks to the following CPBF members who offered valuable suggestions on an earlier draft of this information: Jonathan Hardy, Kathy Lowe, Julian Petley, Sean Tunney and Granville Williams.

The prime targets

Who owns what

By Maggie Brown

To a foreign eye, the British radio market is peculiar and under-developed. Independent local radio only started 30 years ago, 50 years after the BBC. Over the past nine years BBC Radio has strengthened, not weakened its hold. It is nine share points ahead of commercial radio, whose three national networks, Classic FM, TalkSport and Virgin, account for just 8% of total listening. There is no easy commercial entry point, a mainstream rival to Radio 2 or even Radio 1.

Further, there are 21 significant commercial radio owners, 70 overall, of 268 local and regional licences. Yet under the outgoing rules one group can hold up to 15%, which could mean as few as seven owners. Bumping up against the current limit are Capital Radio, Emap (Magic, Kiss) and GWR, with Chrysalis (Heart, Galaxy) on the ascent.

Radio advertising is worth £563m annually, but, along with other media, is becalmed, growing at best by 2% this year. Some 60% is national, but a chunky 27% is local advertising (sponsorship accounts for the remaining 13%). Nor are advertising sales operations concentrated; each big group looks after itself. For foreign moguls, this may add up to a tasty but troublesome snack rather than a meal.

So there are limited choices. Capital Radio, with its coveted London licences, is the purest stock-market opportunity and at the top of buy lists. GWR, owner of Classic FM, has a major shareholder, the Daily Mail & General Trust, holding 27%, which has yet to indicate whether it intends to bid for the lot. Emap is building a multimedia group. Chrysalis, one of the most highly regarded operators, is divesting its TV arm. Scottish Radio Holdings (Radio Clyde, Moray Firth) is part-owned by Scottish Media Group (SMG also owns Virgin Radio).

The Wireless Group, which owns TalkSport, has News International backing and would sit naturally with Sky Sport. The biggest groups are building quasi-national brands focused on British cities and have largely bought their licences from smaller operators.

Radio advertising is worth £563m annually, but, along with other media, is becalmed, growing at best by 2% this year

Lower down the food chain, newspaper groups such as Kent Messenger and Tindle have built up local portfolios. There are other interesting companies, such as UKRD (Pirate Radio).

What is happening is one-off sales of individual licences if the price premium is right, rather than out-and-out takeovers. Also, the Radio Authority has encouraged new owners and formats such as Saga Radio. These operators now face the question of whether they want to sell.

There is bound to be intense competition for big-city licences. The Communications Bill introduces a chance for significant concentration with a plurality rule ensuring a minimum of two owners plus the BBC. Technically, one operator can control 55% of licences in any defined area, but this is overlaid with a strict legal duty to be local. It is also unlikely to happen because of the bite of competition law.

So, stand by for the Radio Bazaar. There are likely to be one or two big takeovers, but a lot of other companies haggling for licences, just as in the final stages of a game of Monopoly.

The Clear Channel CV

Radio and TV

Operates 1,200 US radio stations, with 110m listeners a week and 20% of radio ad spend. Its Premiere Radio Network division syndicates 100 programmes, including the Rush Limbaugh and Dr Laura Schlessinger shows. Owns 36 TV stations in the US and another 250 radio stations in Mexico, Europe and Australasia.

Live entertainment

Via a network of promoters and venues, puts on 26,000 events per year including concerts, Broadway shows, family entertainment, sport.

Sports management

Clear Channel's SFX Sports Group manages and markets sports stars – its UK clients include David Beckham, Steven Gerrard, Alan Hansen, Gary Lineker and Michael Owen.

Outdoor

Owns advertising sites in 65 countries, and claims to reach half of all US adults via highway billboards and ads in malls, airports and city centres.

© *Guardian Newspapers Limited 2003*

UK media ownership

From *Threats on the Landscape – A Survey of who owns what in Europe*

The key media policy issue in the UK is the content of the draft Communications Bill, published in May 2002, which will drastically liberalise media ownership and regulation in the UK, and make the UK the most liberal country, in terms of media ownership rules, in Europe. One controversial proposal is that restrictions on non-EEA ownership of commercial television will be lifted, so that US-based global media groups could acquire commercial TV channels. The other is the lifting of cross-media ownership restrictions, so that potentially, Rupert Murdoch's UK-based News International could acquire the terrestrial commercial television Channel 5. Mid-October 2002 Carlton and Granada announced that they intended to merge.

Many commentators thought the decision to offer Rupert Murdoch a stake in terrestrial television was an attempt by the Labour government, and in particular the Prime Minister, Tony Blair, to keep Murdoch's substantial press interests supportive of the government.

The other controversial proposal in the Bill is to create a monster regulator, OFCOM, which will absorb the functions of five previously separate regulators like the Independent Television Commission (ITC) and the Radio Authority.

There was controversy, too, over the government's reaction to the joint Parliamentary committee of Members of Parliament and the House of Lords, chaired by Lord David Puttnam, set up to scrutinise the Bill. It produced a report, which the government indicated it would ignore, critical of the media ownership changes proposed in the Bill.

England has a very centralised national press, based in London, and produces a range of broadsheet, mid-market and tabloid newspapers. The behaviour of the tabloid press has caused controversy over the years, with its style of intrusive, sensational celebrity and scandal-driven journalism. The newspaper industry is self-regulated by the industry-funded Press Complaints Commission (PCC).

The other nations of the UK – Wales, Northern Ireland, and particularly Scotland – have specific titles catering for readers.

Terrestrial TV and radio

The UK has four principal terrestrial television broadcasters – BBC, ITV, Channel 4 and Channel 5. Over the country as a whole, terrestrial channels still attract 80% of viewing.

BBC

The UK operations of the BBC are funded by the licence fee, which from 2000 up to 2007 will rise annually by 1.5% above inflation. It does not carry any advertising. The BBC broadcasts two national free-to-air channels, BBC1 and BBC 2, five national radio stations and 38 regional radio stations. The combined audience share for the two channels was 35% in summer 2002. In addition, via its BBC Worldwide subsidiary it produces a number of channels for multi-channel television, including BBC Choice, BBC Knowledge and BBC News 24, and publishes magazines such as *BBC Gardener's World*, *Smash Hits* and the *Radio Times*. It has BBC Online, one of the most heavily 'hit' sites in the UK. The BBC also provides the World Service, funded by the UK Foreign and Commonwealth, and it broadcasts in 43 languages.

BBC Worldwide

BBC Worldwide has the responsibility for coordinating commercial operations. This includes the publishing of magazines, videos, DVDs and books as well as programmes. However, the commercial activities do cause controversy. Its planned expansion of educational programming – Curriculum Online, which will create online educational materials free for schools – and the launch of its digital TV channels aimed at children – CBBC and CBeebies – have led educational publishers and commercial broadcasters to complain that they cannot compete fairly with what they see as subsidies from the licence fee to develop new programme areas. BBC News 24 is criticised by Rupert Murdoch for the same reasons. Cable channels in the UK will take BBC News 24, which is free, rather than pay for Sky News.

ITV

The draft Communications Bill clears the way for the creation of a single ITV company. The ITV network consists of fifteen regional franchises, but changes in ownership rules have led to consolidation of ownership, so that two companies have a dominant position, Carlton and Granada, with Scottish Media Group (SMG) in Scotland and Ulster TV in Northern Ireland. Both Carlton and Granada have suffered through the slump in advertising revenue, a fall in the audience share of ITV, and the disastrous failure of the digital terrestrial television (DTT) service, ITV Digital, in which the two companies invested and lost around £31.2 billion until its collapse in March this year. The result has been job losses and cutbacks in both companies.

Carlton

Carlton owns the regional ITV franchises for HTV (Wales and the West of England), London & LLN (the weekday franchise for London), Central (the Midlands), and West Country (the South West). ITV is the biggest commercial television network in UK and franchises consist of ITV1, ITV 2, ITV News Channel and ITV children. Carlton has a 25% stake in GMTV, the breakfast television station, a 20% stake in ITN News and 50% of London News Network. It also has a 7.5% stake in the Spanish digital terrestrial television service, Queiro. Carlton

Productions (ITV producer) includes Planet 24 (entertainment), Action Time (game shows) and Carlton Interactive (online programme). Carlton has also a branch specialised in Production Services with Carlton Studios, Carlton 021, Carlton Post production and Carlton Interactive. Carlton Screen Advertising is cinema advertising sales house. Carlton International is a programme and film sales business with 18,000 hours of television and film. It deals with media rights management, licensing and USA TV movie productions. Carlton operates also in the publishing business with CPG (Carlton Publishing Group). It publishes mainly entertainment, sports and lifestyle books. Carlton Visual Entertainment produces and distributes videos and DVDs for the group.

Granada

Granada is the largest UK commercial broadcaster, owning seven of the fifteen ITV franchises: Anglia, Meridian (South East), Tyne Tees (North East), Yorkshire TV, Granada (North West), Borders (covering the border area with Scotland and the Isle of Man), and the weekend London franchise, LWT.

Granada divides its operations between Granada Platforms (its broadcasting assets) and Granada Content, which include all programme making operations, Granada Film, Granada Sport and Interactive as well as production companies in Australia, North America, Germany and Hong Kong. Granada International is the distribution arm of the group. In 2001, Granada produced 9000 hours of programme for 120 countries. For the ITV network, Granada Content made 2000 hours of programming.

Granada Sky Broadcasting is a joint venture with Sky and it operates two pay-TV channels called Granada Plus and Granada Men and Motors. Granada Media also has a 50% stake in London News Network, a 20% stake in ITN, an 18% stake in the Scottish Media Group, and a 25% stake in GMTV. Other assets include the online search engine Ask Jeeves UK, stakes in two leading football clubs, Liverpool FC (9.9%) and Arsenal FC

(5%), and Manchester United TV. Granada acts as a commercial agent for Arsenal and Liverpool.

Outside the UK, it has a 45% stake in Ireland's fourth national television channel, TV3, and a 10% holding in Channel Seven Network, Australia.

Scottish Media Group (SMG)

A group with interests in radio, newspapers, magazines, television and the internet, but also heavy debts and an uncertain future. It has the ITV franchises for Central (Scottish TV) and North (Grampian TV) Scotland. SMG owns also SMG TV productions and Ginger TV Productions. SMG has a 25% stake in GMTV. SMG is also active in the publishing business with 3 dailies: *The Herald* (95,000), *The Sunday Herald* (167,000) and *The Evening Times* (105,000) and 11 magazines. In the radio sector, SMG operates (Virgin Radio, Virgin Radio Classic, The Groove).

Ulster Television

Broadcasts the ITV franchise for Northern Ireland. Ulster Television is now called UTV. CanWest Global has a 29.9% stake in the franchise. ITV had an audience share of around 30% in summer 2002. UTV entered the radio market with a 60% stake in County Media which operates 4 radio stations. In the UK, UTV has chosen a partner called Absolute Radio UK. UTV acquired also a 50% stake in Bocom international, a supplier of digital broadcasting technologies.

Channel 4

A channel established 20 years ago to appeal to tastes and interests not

catered for by ITV. It also has a public service requirement to produce news, current affairs, schools and other educational-type programmes. It generates revenue by selling its own advertising and through sponsorship. It also makes very few of the programmes it transmits, receiving its news from ITN and commissioning programmes from independent producers. It also has a subscription film channel, FilmFour, and a youth-oriented entertainment channel, E4. However, the channel has had to tackle losses due to falling revenue, and the extra costs of new initiatives. It has an audience share of around 10%.

There is a separate fourth channel in Wales, S4C, which is funded partly by advertising and partly from the state. It carries peak-time Welsh language programmes.

Channel Five

Bertelsmann's RTL have a 65% stake in Channel 5 (United Business Media have the remaining 35%). Its initial problems of coverage have been partially solved – it now is received either through terrestrial or satellite platforms over 85% of the country. Bertelsmann are also repositioning the channel away from its tacky image and it is winning audience share of around 6.5%.

The major problem area has been DTT, where ITV Digital ignominiously collapsed. This has damaged the two companies involved in its development, Carlton and Granada, and also the government's plans to move towards an analogue switch-off. Hopes are now pinned on a re-launch in the autumn, by the BBC and transmitter company Crown Castle, of a new set-top box costing £399, with 24 channels.

Cable, satellite and multimedia

Cable is dominated by two companies, both in a parlous financial state: NTL and Telewest. There is frequent speculation about a merger between the two companies but the level of debt is a problem with NTL's at around £312 billion and Telewest's at £34.4 billion. NTL had about 2.27 million TV customers at the end of 2001.

Liberty Media has a 25% stake in Telewest, and Microsoft 22%. Telewest also own Flextech who have a number of television channels, including a joint venture with the BBC, UK Gold. Telewest had 1.34 million subscribers at the end of 2001.

The real beneficiary of the collapse of ITV Digital, and the uncertainty around cable companies NTL and Telewest, is the home satellite channel, BSkyB, effectively under the control of Rupert Murdoch's News International which has a 37.6% stake in it. The satellite broadcaster's annual results for the year ending 30 June revealed it had 6.1 million subscribers, having added 214,000 subscribers in the last three months (ITV Digital folded in March 2002). After excluding viewers lost through the demise of ITV Digital, this was still a net gain of 148,000. In addition many of the extra subscribers signed up for sports and movies, the most profitable channels for BSkyB. During the same period figures suggest that NTL and Telewest lost about 60,000 customers.

Newspapers

The major characteristic of the UK written press is the existence of a large national newspaper sector. Daily sales in July 2002 totalled 12.3 million, and Sunday sales, 12.5 million. About 60% of people in the UK read a national daily paper, and 70% a national Sunday, but national newspaper sales have declined from the peak sales point of the late 1950s.

The entire national press is owned by seven companies. The four largest of these account for about 90% of sales. They are:

News International
The Sun (3.6 million), *The Times* (632,638), *The News of the World* (3.86 million), *The Sunday Times* (1.3 million).

Trinity Mirror
Daily Mirror (2.1 million), *Daily Record – Scotland* (541,169), *Sunday Mirror* (1.76 million), *The People* (1.3 million), *Sunday Mail – Scotland*.

Daily Mail and General Trust
Daily Mail (2.35 million). *Mail on Sunday* (2.3 million).

Northern and Shell
The *Express* (936,091), *Daily Star* (840,915), *Sunday Express* (926,321).

The other daily national newspapers are *The Daily Telegraph* (946,926), *Financial Times* (432,883), *The Guardian* (375,432) and *The Independent* (191,875), The other Sundays are *The Observer* (411,564 – owned by *The Guardian*), *The Sunday Telegraph* (735,154) and the *Independent on Sunday* (189,742).

Regional newspapers
The regional and local newspaper sector is also highly concentrated. Often groups exchange or purchase titles from each other to establish what are virtually regional monopolies for their titles. The four largest groups are:

Trinity Mirror
Apart from the national newspapers of the Mirror group, acquired through merger in 1999, the group has a total of 234 papers. These include regional dailies, weeklies and free newspapers. It also publishes sports newspapers, including the *Racing Post*.

Newsquest
Owned by the US media group Gannett. Newsquest has 207 titles covering regional dailies, weeklies and free newspapers.

Northcliffe Newspapers
The regional newspaper subsidiary of Daily Mail and General Trust (publishers of the *Daily Mail* and *Mail on Sunday*). It publishes 106 titles.

Johnston Press
Through the acquisition of RIM Johnston moved from fifth to fourth place amongst the top regional publishers. It has 244 titles.

Magazines
German publishing group Bauer target the lower end of the market with magazines like *Take A Break*, *That's Life*, *Bella*, *TV Choice* and *TV Quick*, and a large number of leisure titles, mainly of the puzzle and wordsearch variety.

BBC Worldwide claims to be the UK's third largest consumer magazine publisher, and publishes the UK's most profitable magazine, *Radio Times*.

EMAP (originally East Midlands Allied Press) is an Anglo-French broadcaster and consumer magazine publisher. Its top-selling titles include *FHM*, a men's lifestyle magazine, and *Heat* for women. It organises its magazine publishing in different operating areas, including:

Performance covers both the radio networks Big City, Magic and KISS, music TV channel The Box and music magazines like *Kerrang!*, *mixmag* and *Select*. It also uses these brands to promote CD compilations, club nights, concerts and online activity.

Consumer media handles 30 consumer magazines and websites covering leisure pursuits ranging from golf, fishing to walking and photography. Automotive publishes 28 magazines ranging from *Motor Cycle News* to *Classic Cars*.

EMAP France produces a range of consumer and business magazines and EMAP International supervises the international editions of *FHM*. EMAP France is the publisher of TV guides such as *Tele Star* and *Tele Poche*.

IPC Media Ltd
A major UK magazine publisher, now owned by AOL Time Warner. Publishes two leading women's magazines, *Woman* and *Woman's Own*. Organises its large and varied portfolio of titles under IPC TX (TV, including TV guide, *What's on TV?*), IP Connect (women's fashion, celebrity, teenage), IP Ignite (men's lifestyle) and IPC Country and Leisure (sports, leisure and hobbies).

■ The above information is from *European Media Ownership: Threats on the Landscape – A Survey of who owns what in Europe*, supported by the European Commission
© *European Federation of Journalists*

Media ownership

Information from the Department for Culture, Media and Sport (DCMS)

The Communications Bill will simplify the existing system of media ownership rules. The Bill will deregulate where possible in order to promote competition and attract new investment, ideas and skills. This should lead to increased efficiency and productivity, providing better services to viewers and listeners.

The aim is to retain a balance of different media viewpoints (a 'plurality' of debating voices) in society, and specific limits on the ownership of media assets (over and above competition law thresholds) are the best way to achieve this balance whilst providing the transparency and predictability that minimises costs on business. We will therefore keep those key media ownership rules that act as safeguards of democratic debate, at national, regional and local level.

General disqualifications: rules we will keep

- Political organisations will not be allowed to hold broadcasting licences of any kind.
- Religious organisations will not be allowed to hold any Channel 3 or Channel 5 licence or any national radio analogue licence. They will also be disqualified from holding multiplex licences.

Changes to the ownership rules:

The Communication Bill will:
- Remove the disqualifications on ownership of Broadcasting Act licences by non-EEA persons and advertising agencies; and removes some but not all of the current disqualifications in respect of religious bodies.
- Lift the ban on local authorities holding licences so as to allow them to broadcast information about their services or the services of bodies with similar functions.
- Repeal the two rules which prevent the joint ownership of Channel 3. These are the rules that limit ITV licence holders to no more than 15% of the TV audience, and which prevent the same company from holding the two London licences. The way will be clear for a single ITV, subject to the competition authorities being satisfied that a merger would not be anti-competitive.
- Remove all ownership rules for Channel 5, which could now attract investment from any company.

Within individual media markets

- Local radio ownership rules should ensure that wherever there is a well-developed choice of radio services there will be at least two separate owners of local commercial radio services, in addition to the BBC.
- No one will be allowed to own more than one local digital multiplex in any area (most areas will only have one or two).
- TV – existence of BBC and C4 ensures at least three separate free-to-air broadcasters, plus other platforms.
- Nominated news provider system guarantees quality and independence of ITV news.
- ITV companies will have to ensure the service is adequately financed, to ensure that it is of high quality.
- No one will be allowed to own more than 40% of any nominated news provider, and ITV companies may own no more than 40% in combination or in total.
- Power for the Secretary of State to introduce the system for Channel 5, if that channel's share of the audience for television broadcasting services is broadly equivalent to that of the services comprising Channel 3.

- Power also to revoke the whole arrangement, if a wider range of competitors emerge.

Cross-media ownership rules

- A national '20%' rule:
a) no one controlling more than 20% of the national newspaper market may hold any licence for Ch 3
b) no one controlling more than 20% of the national newspaper market may hold more than a 20% stake in any Ch 3 service
c) a company may not own more than a 20% share in such a service if more than 20% of its stock is in turn owned by a national newspaper proprietor with more than 20% of the market.
- A parallel, regional '20%' rule: no one owning a regional Channel 3 licence may own more than 20% of the local/regional newspaper market in the same region.
- Rules on local radio ownership will ensure there are at least three local/regional commercial media voices (in TV, radio and newspapers) in addition to the BBC in developed markets.

Review

OFCOM will be required to review all media ownership rules at least every three years. They will make any recommendations for further reform to the Secretary of State, who will be able to amend or remove rules by secondary legislation.

Content regulation will ensure the quality, impartiality and diversity of broadcast programming.

Competition law will tend to encourage dispersed ownership and new entry.

■ The above information is from the Department for Culture, Media and Sport's web site which can be found at www.culture.gov.uk

© Crown copyright

TV ad rules to be relaxed this year, says Ofcom chief

The chairman of the new communications super-regulator Ofcom has confirmed that the regulation of television advertising is likely to be relaxed later this year, opening the door for other media sectors to police themselves.

Lord Currie said the onus was on the advertising industry to come up with a scheme that could be overseen by Ofcom.

But he stopped short of referring to self-regulation, speaking instead of a 'co-regulatory' system that would give Ofcom the power to step in if necessary.

> **Ofcom has confirmed that the regulation of television advertising is likely to be relaxed later this year, opening the door for other media sectors to police themselves.**

'If the industry can come up with a scheme that can be audited effectively, Ofcom would be inclined to move towards co-regulation. We will be open to suggestion as to when these opportunities might arise,' Lord Currie told the Oxford Media Convention.

The advertising industry has been lobbying hard for change but the proposals will alarm consumer campaigners, who have expressed concern about the standards of TV advertising.

At present television adverts must be pre-vetted by the broadcast advertising clearance centre, which makes sure they comply with the strict code laid down by the current regulator, the Independent Television Commission.

However, the ITC can intervene to investigate any issues raised by viewers or commercial competitors on issues of taste and decency.

Under the proposed system, the industry would set up its own regulator along the lines of the Advertising Standards Authority, which polices non-broadcast advertising.

In the past year the ITC has overruled several BACC decisions, including issuing a rare public rebuke for clearing an advert for Microsoft's X-Box game console that showed a boy ageing rapidly before crashing into a grave.

Under the new scheme, Ofcom, which will come into force this autumn and replace the five existing media and telecoms regulators, would not take an active role in regulation but would regularly audit the new body to ensure standards were being maintained.

Lord Currie added that Ofcom would seek to extend this 'light touch' co-regulatory approach as far as possible, seeking wherever appropriate to allow media and telecoms industries to regulate themselves.

'The act enjoins us to look for co-regulatory opportunities in other areas and Ofcom is keen to pursue these opportunities,' he said, citing the ASA and the online child protection body the Internet Watch Foundation as possible models for future co-regulatory bodies.

He stressed again the organisation would seek to work with industry to have an approach that was 'co-regulatory and deregulatory where possible', but where necessary would 'intervene decisively and fairly'.

Lord Currie, who yesterday conducted the final round of interviews for the post of Ofcom chief executive, said a decision would be made on an appointment by the end of the month.

Former NTL managing director Stephen Carter is thought to be the frontrunner for the post, with ITC chief executive Patricia Hodgson, McKinsey consultant Nick Lovegrove and BBC Worldwide chief Rupert Gavin tipped as the other names on the shortlist.

© *Guardian Newspapers Limited 2003*

Ofcom

About Ofcom

Ofcom is being designed to be a world-class regulator for the UK's converging communications sector. At the end of 2003, the new Office of Communications will merge the functions of five existing regulatory bodies: the Independent Television Commission (ITC), the Broadcasting Standards Commission (BSC), the Office of Telecommunications (Oftel), the Radio Authority (RAu) and the Radiocommunications Agency (RA).

What Ofcom will do

Ofcom's remit comes from the Office of Communications Act 2002 which gives the organisation the statutory function of preparing for the new regulatory arrangements. These are set out in the Communications Act 2003 which sets out the following general duties:

- To further the interests of consumers in relevant markets
- To secure the optimal use of the radio spectrum
- To ensure that a wide range of television and radio services is available in the UK, comprising high-quality services of broad appeal
- To protect the public from any offensive or potentially harmful effects of broadcast media, and to safeguard people from being unfairly treated in television and radio programmes.

In carrying out these duties, Ofcom will:

- ensure effective delivery of customers' and consumers' needs
- offer an integrated approach to communications regulation
- provide consistency of approach
- deliver clarity of policy
- have the ability to respond flexibly
- strive to maintain diversity and quality within the communications sector
- take forward the expertise of existing regulators
- aim to deliver faster complaints resolution, licence issuing and policy decisions.

Ofcom will also:

- be a vibrant and effective organisation
- provide joined-up regulation
- be flexible and be responsive to the changing realities of the communications sector
- be an integrated regulator
- ensure quality, diversity and choice of content
- deliver decisions which will be clear and with transparent reasons.

As a regulator Ofcom will:

- favour light-handed regulation but intervene when necessary
- create the conditions in which dynamic, vibrant industries can develop
- protect public service broadcasting
- use competition rather than regulation wherever possible to deliver what customers want
- help create a more efficient market
- ensure a wide range and diversity of services
- make decisions based on strong evidence and powerful analysis.

To ensure accountability Ofcom will:

- operate openly and transparently, consulting widely amongst those affected by its decisions
- establish a consumer panel
- establish a content board
- build relationships across the communications sector
- establish a presence across the UK
- develop a range of activities – public meetings, seminars and conferences to ensure interaction with citizens and consumers.

How will Ofcom regulate?

Ofcom will:

- take over the functions of the statutory bodies and office holders that currently regulate the electronic communications sector
- encourage effective self-regulation and co-regulation, with a streamlined and integrated strategic approach
- replace the current system of licensing for telecommunications systems with a new framework for the regulation of electronic communications networks and services
- as part of its wider spectrum management duties, Ofcom will have the power to develop new mechanisms to enable spectrum to be traded in accordance with regulations made by Ofcom, and a scheme of recognised spectrum access
- develop the current system for regulating broadcasting to reflect technological change, to accommodate the switchover from analogue to digital broadcasting, and to rationalise the regulation of public service broadcasters
- establish a Consumer Panel to advise and assist Ofcom and to represent and protect consumer interests
- establish a Content Board to advise Ofcom on a wide range of content issues as they affect viewers, listeners and citizens, predominantly dealing with broadcasting but also responsible for the development of media literacy.
- exercise concurrently powers under the Competition Act 1998 and the Enterprise Act 2002 across the whole of the communications sector (including broadcasting)
- establish procedures for appeal of decisions relating to networks and services and rights of use for spectrum.

What will Ofcom do?

Ofcom's remit affects a broad section of industry and public stakeholders. Ofcom intends to consult widely when formulating its policies, to ensure we make the appropriate decisions on major regulatory issues. Ofcom is expected to launch a consultation on its main business principles in spring 2003.

- The above information is from Ofcom's web site which can be found at www.ofcom.org.uk

© Ofcom 2003

The advertising media

Information from the Advertising Association

Advertisements are messages intended to inform or influence the people who receive them. If there is no one to receive the message, there is no point in sending it. This briefing is about the advertising media – the places where advertisements appear.

In Britain the main media for advertising are the Press and television. Others include direct mail, posters, Internet, Commercial Radio, the cinema, showcards and other advertising material in shops and 'novelty' items such as beer mats and coasters, T-shirts and key rings. Things are different in other countries. In the United States, for example, radio is a far more important advertising medium than it is here. In India, where there are few TV sets but millions go to see films each week, the cinema is important to advertisers. Before Independent Television started in Britain in 1955, the Press was well ahead as the most important medium, and the cinema was next.

The Press

The Press – newspapers and magazines – makes up the largest group of media. In Britain it is usually divided into:

- The national newspapers. 14 daily and 11 Sunday newspapers which are distributed all over England and Wales, and in most cases also in Scotland. Most of the Sunday papers include a 'free' colour magazine.
- Regional morning and evening newspapers. There are 18 regional morning papers, 72 regional evening papers and 7 regional Sunday papers.
- Local weekly papers. There are about 477 of these, some with tiny circulations of only 1000 or so. The total is larger if you count all the different editions of what is substantially the same newspaper.
- Free distribution publications. These are distributed free from door to door. There are many hundreds of them, most of them covering a group of suburbs or part of a large city.
- Consumer magazines. The BBC's *Radio Times* and *TV Times*, are in this group. So are the weekly and monthly women's magazines, the magazines for teenagers and magazines for men.
- Special interest magazines. Whatever your interest is, from angling to keeping caged birds, from hot rod cars to bell ringing, you can be sure that there is at least one weekly or monthly magazine to suit you. Consumer and special interest magazines, put together, total over 3,500.
- Business and professional magazines. Grocers, teachers, electronics engineers, doctors, nurses, builders and plumbers all have their own newspapers or magazines. So does almost anyone you can think of, whatever job they do. There are over 6,300 titles serving this very diverse market.
- Controlled circulation magazines. These cannot be bought from newsagents. They are posted to members of certain professions or trades and carry advertising of interest to their particular readership.

So, taking newspapers and magazines together, there are well over 10,000 different regular publications in the UK available to the advertiser. The advertisers can talk to several million people by advertising in one of the popular national newspapers or in the TV programme magazines. If they have a particular message for people who keep pet rabbits or make model aircraft, it can be put in one of the special interest magazines. If the aim is to reach members of a particular trade or profession, advertisements can be put in the business and professional magazines. And if the advertiser wants to get in touch with people who live in a specific region or a rural area, space can be bought in the local paper.

In the UK, a popular daily newspaper like *The Sun* sells nearly 4 million copies every day or the *Daily Mirror* nearly 2.5 million per day. The *Radio Times* sells about 1.4 million copies a week. The *Financial Times* sells 385,000 copies every day, just less than the monthly *Ideal Home*. Two weekly women's magazines, *Woman's Own* and *Woman*, each sells around 630,000 copies. At the other end of the scale, many technical and business magazines, and many local papers, sell only a few thousand copies of each issue. But the number of copies sold does not tell the whole story, for two reasons:

- Readership – the total number of people who read each issue – is sometimes more important than circulation – the number of copies sold. For example the *Radio Times* stays in the house for a whole week and is looked at by everyone in the house who can read. So its readership is actually close to 5 million, i.e. for every copy sold there are more than three readers. There is another aspect of readership. Some magazines, especially the glossy monthly magazines, tend to be passed on when the original buyer has read them.
- The buying power of a newspaper's or magazine's readership is also important. For example, you would reach more people who might buy a Rolls-Royce car by advertising in the *Financial Times*,

> *In Britain the main media for advertising are the Press and television. Others include direct mail, posters, Internet and Commercial Radio*

despite its relatively small circulation, than readers of the *Sun* who are more likely than those of the *Financial Times* to be interested in a small saving on grocery prices.

Television

In the UK, ITV (including GMTV), Channel 4 and Channel 5 (1997), show advertisements between programmes and in intervals within the programmes themselves. These are the three commercial television channels licensed and regulated by the Independent Television Commission. The programmes are broadcast by the 15 programme companies (two for the London area and one for each of the 13 other regions) that make up the ITV Network, plus GMTV and Channel 4. The companies and GMTV sell advertising time, and the money they receive pays for the programmes they show on ITV and Channels 4 and 5. Only seven minutes of each hour, on average, may be given over to advertisements, with the maximum allowed at peak time of seven and a half minutes. On satellite and cable TV the limit is an average of nine minutes per hour over a day.

Advertising time on TV is sold in 'spots' ranging from one minute down to seven seconds. Daytime spots, when audiences are low, cost less than those in 'peak time' – the evening – when millions of people may be watching Independent Television. Since January 1991, television programmes have been eligible for sponsorship, details of which are set down in the Independent Television Commission's Code of Programme Sponsorship.

The regional basis of Independent Television means that an advertiser can put across his message nationally, in a number of regions or in only one region. It also enables him to 'test market' a product – or an advertising campaign – in only one region before launching it nationally. The two BBC channels do not carry paid advertising, but between programmes they show promotional material for future programmes, for books and records associated with programmes, for the BBC's weekly listings magazine, *Radio Times*, as well

as Public Service Announcements by the Central Office of Information.

Radio

The public service organisation in the United Kingdom, the BBC (44 stations), does not take advertising. However, there are now over 240 commercial stations, licensed and regulated by the Radio Authority, that pay for themselves by taking money from advertising. There are now national, regional and local commercial stations broadcasting.

Commercial Radio stations, unlike TV stations, are no longer restricted to a limit on how much advertising they can take per hour – however, they generally stick to the old limit of nine minutes, because too much advertising causes listeners to tune elsewhere. As with television, radio advertising time is sold on a 'spot' basis. Peak audience times are different, however, with radio audiences largest in the breakfast period and the evening rush-hour. Sponsorship is a growing method of communication on radio, and is not bound by the tightness of regulations that TV is subject to.

Commercial Radio covers virtually the whole of the UK. In larger areas of population such as the major conurbations, there are multiple commercial options – in London you can choose from 17 different commercial services, as well as all the BBC services. This will continue in other areas, as the remit of the Radio Authority is to extend listener choice, by licensing stations that offer something different from those already broadcasting.

Outdoor advertising

Poster sites in Britain are mainly in the big cities and alongside main roads close to the cities. Outdoor advertising also includes the sides and backs of buses, banners and boards at football and other sports events, both the inside and outside of London and other city taxis, bus shelters, and boards at bus and railway stations.

Except for posters at bus shelters and stations, where waiting passengers may have time to react, the message on a poster has to be very simple. Many people will see it from a passing bus or car, and no one is going to stop in the street to read a poster. So posters are often used to remind people of brand names, or tie in with TV advertising to remind people of the TV message.

Direct mail

This is advertising that is brought to our door by the postman, addressed to you by name. It may consist of a fairly long letter describing the goods or services on offer, together with a leaflet with more details, a coupon and post-paid envelope for your reply and often information about a competition or 'lucky draw' to get you interested. Books and records are often advertised by this method.

If advertisers sent direct mail letters to everyone, a huge number of letters would be wasted. So there are companies which sell lists of names and addresses of people known to be interested in certain subjects. For example, if you wanted to advertise a book about stamps, you could buy a list of stamp-collectors.

Leaflet distribution

Leaflets are sometimes brought round by the postman and sometimes by other distributors. They are not personally addressed, and, to save costs, several leaflets are sometimes distributed together. These might include a local leaflet from a building firm, a regional leaflet from a company selling double-glazing, and a national leaflet containing a 5p off soap offer.

Point of sale

Point of sale (POS) advertising includes posters for the shop window, complete window displays for the advertiser's products, 'Open' and 'Closed' notices for the door with a product name on them, and the various other small advertising items that you see in shops. These are sometimes part of a short-term advertising campaign, but more often they are used to keep an advertiser's name in the minds of shoppers.

Cinema

Since the 1950s, when television became the most popular form of entertainment for most people in Britain, fewer people have gone to the cinema regularly. Numbers of admissions declined to 54 million by 1985 but have since picked up again to 135 million in 1998. Many local cinemas with a single screen have closed, but instead, bigger complexes with many screens serving larger areas have become more common. In 1998 there were nearly 2700 screens. Consequently, cinema advertising has become less important in overall media reach terms. However, today's cinema audience tends to include a high proportion of young people in the 15-24 age-range who live in or near cities and have money to spend.

Summing up

Taken all together, the media make it possible for the advertiser to reach the whole population or any part of it, from large groups to small ones. One of the skills that goes into successful advertising is finding the right 'mix' of media for the advertiser's purpose.

■ The above information is from the Advertising Association's web site which can be found at www.adassoc.org.uk

© The Advertising Association

Press self-regulation

A brief history. Information from the Press Complaints Commission

The creation of a voluntary Press Council in 1953 heralded the beginning of press self-regulation. The aim was to maintain high ethical standards of journalism and to promote press freedom.

However, during the 1980s, a small number of publications failed in the view of many to observe the basic ethics of journalism. This in turn, reinforced a belief among many members of Parliament that the Press Council, which had lost the confidence of some in the press, was not a sufficiently effective body. Some of them believed that the public interest required the enactment of a law of privacy and a right of reply as well as a statutory press council wielding enforceable legal sanctions.

Given the serious implications of such a course of action, the Government appointed a Departmental Committee under David Calcutt QC to consider the entire matter. The terms of reference were:

To consider what measures (whether legislative or otherwise) are needed to give further protection to individual privacy from the activities of the press and improve recourse against the press for the individual citizen, taking account of existing remedies, including the law on defamation and breach of confidence; and to make recommendations.

The Report of the Calcutt Committee was published in June 1990. It recommended the setting up of a new Press Complaints Commission in place of the Press Council. The new Commission would have eighteen months to demonstrate 'that non-statutory self-regulation can be made to work effectively. This is a stiff test for the press. If it fails, we recommend that a statutory system for handling complaints should be introduced.'

The press responded with vigour to the report and acted with great speed and co-operation to set up an independent Press Complaints Commission at the beginning of 1991.

A Committee of national and regional editors produced for the very first time a Code of Practice for the new Press Complaints Commission to uphold. All publishers and editors committed themselves to this and to

ensuring secure and adequate funding of the PCC. A Press Standards Board of Finance (Pressbof), modelled on the self-regulatory system established by the advertising industry in 1974, was put in place and charged with raising a levy upon the newspaper and periodical industries to finance the Commission. This arrangement ensures secure financial support for the PCC, while its complete independence is at the same time guaranteed by a majority of lay members, and is a further sign of the industry's commitment to effective self-regulation.

Over the past few years, the PCC has continued to grow in stature – building on the accomplishments of its early years. In 1995 the then Government recognised the achievements of the PCC in making effective press self-regulation in its White Paper *Privacy and Media Intrusion*.

The Labour Government, elected in 1997, has also made clear its support for effective self-regulation and for the work of the Press Complaints Commission. To date, the Commission has handled nearly 30,000 complaints.

■ The above information is from the Press Complaints Commission's web site which can be found at www.pcc.org.uk

© Press Complaints Commission

Students' frequently asked questions by answered

Why doesn't the PCC impose fines? Isn't the publication of adjudications a fairly weak response to what are quite often serious complaints?

As a non-statutory body the Commission does not have the power to impose fines, which would inevitably entail lawyers for complainants and legal powers for the complaints handling body. The PCC would have to be given legal powers by statute with all the drawbacks – such as costs, delay and risk – inherent in that, as well as the implications for press freedom. In any case, it is doubtful that fines would be at all effective. Evidence from overseas suggests that where fines do exist (for example in France) editors risk publishing intrusive stories – and then pay the damages – because the increase in sales more than compensates for the cost of the fine. Awards by the European Court of Human Rights for breaches of privacy limit payouts to around £10,000, which is a fairly small sum for large, successful newspapers.

On the other hand, critical adjudications of the PCC must be published in full and with due prominence, meaning that editors have to publicise to their staff, rivals and readers that they have broken the rules agreed by all editors. Such a sanction – which calls into question an editor's professional judgement – is a far greater deterrent than fines. Adjudications can run to a full newspaper or magazine page which has its own financial implications resulting from the loss of potential advertising space. Furthermore, most editors have adherence to the Code written into their contracts of employment – meaning that, in cases of a serious breach, the Commission can draw the attention of the editor's employer to an adjudication. Breaches of the Code can therefore be a disciplinary matter within newspapers.

To illustrate the effectiveness of the sanction, the Commission draws attention to the fact that very few breaches of the Code have to be adjudicated. Editors will go out of their way to resolve complaints to the satisfaction of the complainant if they think there is any danger that they will lose an adjudication. This means that complainants get very quick and effective redress – far quicker and more useful than any legal system could deliver, and far quicker than would be the case if the process was diverted by haggling over the level of any fine. It is interesting to note that complaints made through lawyers – a foretaste of what any statutory system would be like – take up to 150% longer to deal with than complaints made directly to the Commission.

If the Code is written by the industry and self-regulation, including the running of the PCC, is funded by the industry, how can the PCC's judgements on complaints under the Code be impartial?

The importance of the Code as a document written by and for editors is explained above. Briefly, it is essential to the workings of self-regulation and to the power of adjudication that, if found against, the editor of a publication must admit publicly that the rules to which they have contributed and by which they have agreed to abide have been broken. Similarly, the fact that the

industry funds the PCC ensures that not only is no financial burden placed upon the taxpayer or complainants, but that each newspaper group is committed to the ideal of self-regulation.

However, the make-up of the Commission reflects the fact that, while it is supported by the industry, it is also – crucially – independent from it. The Chairman of the PCC is always a figure from outside the world of journalism and the Commission itself has a majority of lay members, themselves independently appointed. These are respected people from a variety of other industries, who bring not only wide-ranging experience of different walks of life but also are removed from the daily workings of the industry itself. The minority of editors on the Commission bring with them an industry perspective essential to the decision-making process, but they can never dominate proceedings.

Critical adjudications, as well as corrections and apologies in cases of significant inaccuracy, must be published with due prominence. What do you mean by due prominence?

The Commission does not instruct editors where to publish apologies or adjudications, but the requirement in the Code for due prominence means that the Commission expects them to be published somewhere in proportion to the original report. This does not mean necessarily on the same page – it depends on the gravity of the error or intrusion or possibly on the speed with which an error is corrected. It also depends, in cases involving accuracy, on the proportion of the original story that was wrong. Letters pages are a popular way of affording complainants a right to reply, and although they usually appear to the rear of a newspaper they are actually among the most widely-read pages in many newspapers. Some newspapers also have designated corrections columns, or a Readers' Editor, which provide an alternative means of solving disputes and highlighting corrections.

Ultimately, the PCC is a dispute resolution service and seeks to resolve all complaints to the satisfaction of the complainant. The precise location of a published correction or apology can therefore be negotiated as part of this process.

Would it not be better if print and broadcast media all came under the same Code and the same authority?

The print medium is fundamentally different from other media in the manner that it is transmitted and received and it is, therefore, vitally important for it to have a separate regulating body equipped to deal with the particular issues relevant to it. Most importantly, whereas companies require a licence from government to broadcast and therefore are subject to statutory control, newspapers guarantee freedom of expression away from governmental interference and therefore require an independent form of self-regulation – which the PCC provides. This was a point acknowledged by the Government when it amended the Human Rights Act 1998 (in what became Clause 12 of the Act) to protect the position of self-regulation as a manifestation of freedom of expression.

Broadcasting and advertising codes deal with matters of taste and decency. Why does the print editors' Code not do that?

It is universally recognised that a free press is an essential part of a democratic society. The PCC similarly recognises that newspapers must have editorial freedom to publish what they choose so long as the rights of individuals are not compromised by their content. Therefore, provided the stringent terms of the industry's own Code of Practice – designed especially to protect the individual – are not breached, the PCC cannot, and would not wish, to place any limits on editorial selection. If the PCC were to make the very subjective judgement as to whether material is

'tasteless' or 'offensive', it would be assuming the role of moral arbiter, which is ultimately to say censor. Instead, most editors are aware of what is and is not acceptable to their readership and, if miscalculations are made on this score, market forces will generally dictate they are not repeated.

This is an example of why the PCC is different from other media regulators. Advertising billboards, and to a lesser extent television programmes, contain information disseminated on an extremely wide scale, the consumption of which cannot necessarily be controlled. For example, as anyone can look at an advert, it is necessary to ensure that all advertisements do not break basic standards of decency and taste. Newspapers are actively purchased and therefore need not be subject to the same restrictions.

Does the PCC just exist for the rich and famous?

Quite the contrary. The PCC is specifically designed to help members of the public who find themselves – often through no fault of their own – involved in news stories. To this end, the PCC provides a free and accessible service, which requires no legal expertise, and includes: a Helpline to assist members of the public in making complaints; the publication of literature in a range of minority languages – including Welsh, Urdu, Bengali, Gaelic, Arabic, Somali and Chinese; an Internet site so that information is available 24 hours a day; a Textphone to assist deaf or hard-of-hearing

persons with enquiries; and a 24-hour paging service to ensure that personal advice is available around the clock for all those who need it. In 2001 over 90% of all complainants were ordinary members of the public.

Is there any special treatment for Royals?

Complaints by members of the royal family tend to attract a high level of media attention, which may create the erroneous impression that they are dealt with in a different fashion to other complaints. In fact, the same rules under the Code apply to newspapers and magazines when covering the royal family, and the same service is available at the PCC should a complaint subsequently be made.

For example, the PCC has sought to ensure that recent media coverage of Prince William generally affords him the same basic rights, in accordance with the terms of the Code of Practice, as any young person going to school and university. Lord Wakeham, former chairman of the PCC, made clear that 'no one is asking for special treatment and the principles in the Code apply to everyone else as much as him'.

Is the PCC out of step with Europe?

Far from it. In fact, the overwhelming majority of media ethics bodies in Europe are self-regulatory. Only Ireland and France do not have any similar body; and only in Portugal is there a statutory body.

Some of the self-regulatory bodies have long-established roots (the Swedish Press Council for

instance is over eighty-five years old) while others have been more recently set up (a Press Council in Bosnia & Herzegovina was established just three years ago). Moreover, different bodies have slightly different remits and functions – which, given that they are set against different cultural and political backgrounds, is quite proper. Nevertheless, there are around fifteen self-regulatory councils around the continent, all of which seek to maintain press freedom while ensuring press responsibility.

These bodies meet annually and form a loose-knit grouping known as the Alliance of Independent Press Councils of Europe, in which the PCC plays a full part. Delegates are able to find out which issues are facing their counterparts in other countries, give and receive advice and ensure that they are providing the best possible service to the public.

There are also many Press Councils and similar self-regulatory bodies further afield – many of which have been established after seeking advice and help, with the consent of the British Government, from the PCC. A new web site, which can be found at www.presscouncils.org, gives further information on all such bodies around the world. It is a sure sign that the ideals of self-regulation are widely held in high esteem and that countries all over the globe have put those ideals into practice.

How can I get further information?
The Commission's news service emails over 700 parties with an interest in the publishing industry in the UK and around the world every week.

The PCC has provided a detailed response to the DCMS Select Committee Inquiry in Privacy and the Media of 2003, which describes in detail both the process and philosophy of self-regulation, and can be accessed through the web site.

Our 2002 Annual Review is now available. This contains a detailed statistical breakdown of the trends in complaints, analysis of the major issues the Commission has dealt with in the past year and an assessment of press self-regulation in an inter-national context. To be placed on our mailing list to receive a copy, or to get copies from previous years, please email your request to pcc@pcc.org.uk

For a more in-depth study of the Commission's inception in 1991, its history and the status of self-regulation ten years on, a limited number of copies of Professor Richard Shannon's book *A Press Free and Responsible: Self-regulation and the Press Complaints Commission 1991-2001* are available from the Commission at the special student price of £9.50, including postage and packing. Please email your request to pcc@pcc.org.uk

■ The above information is from the Press Complaints Commission's web site which can be found at www.pcc.org.uk

© Press Complaints Commission

Complaints about teenage magazines

How to make a complaint about the coverage of sex-related issues in teenage magazines

If you are unhappy with an article in a teenage magazine, you can make a complaint in the following way:

If you are unhappy with something in the magazine, you should firstly write to the editor of the magazine as it is important for them to know about your concerns.

If you are not completely satisfied with the response from the editor, you can write to TMAP, which is made up of experts from the field of law, public health and child health care and development and also the magazine publishers themselves. It is administered by the Periodical Publishers' Association (PPA), the industry organisation for magazines in the UK.

All complaints will be carefully considered. If a complaint is clearly not in breach of the guidelines your letter will be responded to immediately. All other complaints will be considered at TMAP meetings, held quarterly. They will write to let you know when the next meeting is to be held and that they will respond to your complaint at this time.

If the magazine is considered to be in breach of the guidelines, TMAP will write to the editor of the relevant magazine to inform them of the breach. A copy of this letter will be sent to you.

If the magazine is considered to be in breach of the guidelines, it will be highlighted in TMAP's annual report which will be made available to the Home Office, the publishing industry and other interested parties. You will also be able to obtain a copy.

There is a separate code for advertising which is produced by the Committee of Advertising Practice (CAP) and complaints are adjudicated by the Advertising Standards Authority (ASA). The ASA will make the final decisions on any complaints about advertising within teenage magazines.

Examples of teenage magazines regulated by the guidelines include:
Bliss (Emap Elan), *Mizz* (IPC Magazines), *Smash Hits* (EMAP Metro), *J17* (EMAP Elan), *Sugar* (Attic Futura), *TV Hits* (Attic Futura).

To contact the TMAP and for a copy of the guidelines or annual report please write to: TMAP, c/o Periodical Publishers' Association (PPA), Queens House, 28 Kingsway, London WC2B 6JR. Tel: 020 7405 0819. Fax: 020 7404 4167.

TMAP is a self-regulating body whose remit is to ensure that the guidelines are adhered to. Breaches are highlighted in a formal way ensuring that mistakes are unlikely to happen again.

• The above information is from the Teenage Magazine Arbitration Panel's web site which can be found at www.ppa.co.uk/tmap

© The Teenage Magazine Arbitration Panel (TMAP)

Privacy law is 'best way' to protect the public

By Tom Leonard, Media Editor

The Government was urged to reconsider its opposition to a privacy law yesterday after an all-party committee of MPs concluded that existing regulations failed to protect the public from media intrusion.

The Commons culture, media and sport select committee said it was clear that if politicians failed to create a privacy law to conform with the provisions of the Human Rights Act, judges would do it piecemeal for them in the courts.

It said a law was needed to 'clarify the protection that individuals can expect from unwarranted intrusion by anyone – not the press alone – into their private lives'.

In its eagerly awaited report on privacy and media intrusion, the committee called for the existing system of newspaper self-regulation to be more strict.

The Press Complaints Commission had met with some success in improving press behaviour but was 'slightly too softly, softly' and should have enhanced powers and a tougher code of conduct, said MPs.

The Government indicated last night that it would still oppose a privacy law but stressed it was 'very important that the PCC takes the opportunity to reform very seriously'.

Committee members faced hostile questioning from tabloid journalists at a press conference yesterday but insisted they were not trying to undermine press freedom or the principle of self-regulation.

'I support a free press but I don't believe in a free for all press', said Chris Bryant, the Labour MP for Rhondda.

The report rejected calls for the PCC to be made answerable to Ofcom, the new statutory communications super-regulator.

Among the report's wide-ranging recommendations were fines for newspapers that broke the PCC code, an annual league table showing the best and worst offenders, and front-page apologies.

> **'The Government continues to believe that a free press is vital in a democracy and that self-regulation is the best regulatory system'**

MPs said the code should 'explicitly ban' payments to the police for information as well as ban the use and payment of intermediaries such as private detectives.

The report expressed surprise that the PCC had failed to investigate an admission to the committee by the *Sun*'s editor, Rebekah Wade, that such payments had been made to police.

MPs said the PCC, which has been accused in the past of being a 'cosy editor's club', would command more confidence in the independence of its membership if it advertised openly for its lay members rather than – as had happened in the past – recruiting friends.

Press members who presided over 'persistently offending publications' should be forced to stand down, said the report.

An independent figure should be appointed to consider appeals and commission a regular audit of the PCC's processes and practices.

The PCC's code committee, which draws up the journalistic code of conduct, should no longer be composed merely of editors but also include lay members.

The MPs also said they wanted to see the PCC, which usually only acts after a complaint is made, take a more pro-active approach and warn newspapers before they offended.

'The PCC, as seen very recently, finds no difficulty in intervening, justifiably, to protect the privacy of Prince William; surely there are other deserving recipients of its concern,' the report said.

Commenting on the report, the PCC's new chairman, Sir Christopher Meyer, repeated his view that the PCC 'works better through "self-regulation plus" – a commission in which tough-minded lay members outnumber editors – than any alternative on offer'.

He said the PCC would read the report carefully but was not obliged to any accept any recommendations.

Tessa Jowell, the Culture Secretary, said: 'The Government continues to believe that a free press is vital in a democracy and that self-regulation is the best regulatory system. That does not mean that there is no room for improvement.'

Privacy law

Privacy law needed to protect journalistic freedom and individual privacy

A new privacy law is needed to clarify journalists' right to investigate, according to the Institute for Public Policy Research (ippr). Following the publication of the Culture, Media and Sport select committee report, ippr argues that the failure of media self-regulation and interpretations of the Human Rights Act have created uncertainty about journalistic freedom and individuals' rights to privacy.

ippr's report, *Ruled by Recluses*, published last November warned that without a radical reform of self-regulation and greater clarity on privacy laws, the UK could end up with the worst of both worlds: courts interpreting the Human Rights Act in a way that only benefits the rich and famous and journalists' freedoms being curbed unnecessarily.

ippr recommends a review of what is understood to be in the public interest and wants the Government to consider introducing legislation on privacy in the next parliament.

Jamie Cowling, ippr Research Fellow, said:

'Privacy cases brought under the Human Rights Act, such as the Sara Cox case, demonstrate that regulation of the media badly needs an overhaul. Journalists are facing confusion and uncertainty about their rights to investigate. There is a real danger that we will see the right to privacy defined on the basis of the legal challenges of a privileged few celebrities.

'There is an urgent need for a real debate about the notion of public interest: the fact that a lot of people are interested in the private lives of others does not alone provide sufficient reason for publishing. What is needed is a framework which will protect freedom of the media to investigate in the public interest whilst ensuring that the right to privacy is accessible for all regardless of income.'

Additional recommendations:
- Journalists must reaffirm their commitment to providing quality news of genuine importance and undertake to intrude into personal privacy only to report matters that will have a genuine impact on people's lives.
- All newspapers should appoint a readers' ombudsman to deal with complaints.
- Government must monitor case law and regulatory adjudication on media privacy and appoint an independent panel to review it in 2004.

The current broadcast and press regulators should:
- Affirm the principles of the Human Rights Act and modify their codes to comply with its provisions, and to cover new surveillance technologies.
- Affirm their commitment to protecting privacy, perhaps by introducing tougher sanctions including fines against media who intrude on an individual's privacy for no good reason.
- Reform or design new procedures to ensure that their actions are transparent and publicly accountable.
- Ensure an adequate balance between lay people and experts on adjudication panels. Both are needed if a regulator is to keep in touch with the public mood as well as sensitive to media issues.

Notes:
- *Ruled by Recluses* was the result of a twelve-month research project and includes essays from: Prof. Eric Barendt, Professor of Media Law, UCL; Lord Dubs, Chairman, BSC; Rabinder Singh QC and James Strachan, Gray's Inn, all of whom were called as witnesses to the Culture, Media and Sport Select Committee Inquiry. *Ruled by Recluses* also included evidence from, Prof. David Morrison and Michael Svennevig, University of Leeds, and Lord Wakeham's final publication as Chairman of the PCC.
- *Ruled by Recluses: Privacy, Journalism and the Media after the Human Rights Act* by Damian Tambini and Clare Heyward is available by post or email from the ippr media office (journalists only) or from Central Books: 0845 458 9911.

■ The above information is from the Institute for Public Policy Research's web site which can be found at www.ippr.org.uk

© Institute for Public Policy Research (IPPR)

Taste and decency

Information from the Radio Authority

Key points

- Whilst matters of taste and decency do not lend themselves to hard-and-fast rules, there is general agreement on the need to show sensitivity in the treatment of particular issues, especially when these involve children and young people;
- The Broadcasting Act 1990 requires the Radio Authority to do all it can to ensure that 'nothing shall be included in programmes which offends against good taste or decency, or is likely to encourage or incite to crime or to lead to disorder or to be offensive to public feeling';
- The Authority has issued Codes on News and Current Affairs, Programming, Advertising and Sponsorship. These are available at the Authority's website (www.radioauthority.org.uk);
- The News and Current Affairs and Programme Codes set out general principles that apply, primarily in relation to young listeners, imitated behaviour, language, bad taste, sexual matters, portrayal of violence, crime, terrorism and anti-social behaviour, smoking, drinking and drugs;
- The Authority's Advertising and Sponsorship Code sets out similar guidelines for the handling of advertising. In particular advertisements must avoid using material or themes likely to cause general offence or denigrate particular group;
- Special care must be taken in the handling of religious issues.

Background

The Broadcasting Act 1990, Section 90(1)(a), requires the Radio Authority to do all it can to ensure that 'nothing shall be included in programmes which offends against good taste or decency, or is likely to encourage or incite to crime or to lead to disorder or to be offensive to

public feeling'. Whilst this is an area that does not lend itself to hard-and fast-rules, there are a number of areas where there is general acceptance that rules and guidance can help stations to avoid creating offence.

To help stations meet their obligations under the Act, the Authority has issued Codes on News and Current Affairs, Programming, Advertising and Sponsorship which set out in plain English the requirements of the legislation. The Codes are available at the Authority's web site (www.radioauthority.org.uk) The News and Current Affairs and Programme Codes set out general principles that apply, primarily in relation to young listeners, imitated behaviour, language, bad taste, sexual matters, portrayal of violence, crime, terrorism and anti-social behaviour, smoking, drinking and drugs.

Young listeners

Section 91(2) of the Broadcasting Act, 1990 requires the Authority to 'have special regard to programmes included in licensed services in circumstances such that large numbers of children and young persons may be expected to be listening to programmes'. Stations need to be vigilant, and sensitive to the problems, and have regard to the following points:

- for the purposes of the Code, young persons are taken to be those under 18 years of age;
- the timing of broadcast of adult material should take account of research and avoid times when there may be expected to be significant numbers of young listeners;
- programming specifically directed at a young audience must take care to avoid content such as strong language, explicit news reports, discussion or phone-ins which cover explicit violent or sexual topics in a frank manner, musical items with violent or sexually explicit lyrics.

Imitated behaviour

The portrayal or description of dangerous behaviour easily imitated by children must not be broadcast when children are likely to be listening.

Language in programming

The gratuitous use of offensive

language, including blasphemy, must be avoided. Bad language and blasphemy must not be used in programmes aimed at young listeners, or when audience research indicates they might be expected to be listening in significant numbers.

There is no absolute rule on the use of bad language, but its use must be defensible in terms of context and authenticity. Where lyrics in songs might cause offence, stations are expected to make considered judgements having regard to scheduling (particularly bearing in mind listener sensitivity to 'school run' times).

Bad taste in humour

We do all we can to make sure that stations avoid humour which offends against good taste or decency, particularly where this is based on particular characteristics like race, gender or disability. Jokes can all too easily exploit or humiliate for the purpose of entertainment. This can both hurt those most directly concerned and repel many listeners. Racist terms should be avoided, as should insensitive comments and stereotyped portrayals.

Sexual matters

The same considerations apply here as to bad language. Entertainment and comedy have often relied on sexual innuendo, but this does not justify gratuitous crudity, the portrayal of perversion, sexism or the degradation of either sex. Music and art are often concerned with love and passion, and it would be wrong (and impossible) to require writers or lyricists not to shock or disturb. The aim should be to move, not offend.

Sexual and other offences involving children

When covering any pre-trial investigation into an alleged criminal offence in the UK, stations need to pay particular regard to the potentially vulnerable position of any person under 18 involved as a witness or a victim before broadcasting anything likely to identify them. Particular justification is also required for revealing the same information about any person under 18 who is a defendant or a potential defendant.

We do all we can to make sure that stations avoid humour which offends against good taste or decency

---

Portrayal of violence

Violence must never be glorified or applauded. The portrayal of violence is addressed in the Broadcasting Act 1990, which requires the Radio Authority to draw up a Code giving guidance 'as to the rules to be observed with respect to the inclusion in programmes of sounds suggestive of violence, particularly in circumstances such that large numbers of children and young persons may be expected to be listening to the programmes' and to ensuring the exclusion of material which 'offends against good taste and decency' or 'is likely to be offensive to public feeling'.

Crime, terrorism and anti-social behaviour

Section 90 of the Broadcasting Act 1990 requires the Radio Authority to do all that it can to ensure that 'nothing is broadcast which . . . is likely to encourage or incite to crime or lead to disorder or to be offensive to public feeling'.

Any interview with criminals needs to be justified as being in the public interest. Apart from the requirements of the 1990 Act, other legal considerations must be borne in mind (e.g. if the interviewee is known to be wanted by the police, or has escaped from jail). No payment should be made to a criminal whose sentence has not yet been discharged. Former criminals should not be paid for interviews about their crimes unless an important public interest is served.

All plans for programmes which explore and expose the views of people who use or advocate the use of violence for the achievement of political ends must be considered carefully by senior management before any arrangements for broadcasting are made.

Smoking/drinking/drugs

Care is needed with programming likely to be heard by young people, and those directed at that age group should not normally contain any reference to smoking or drinking of alcohol unless an educational point is being made. Drugs, drug addiction and their effects are valid subjects for radio programming, but no impression should be given that drug taking is desirable. The same applies to solvent abuse, and descriptions of such practices that could easily be imitated must be avoided.

Advertising

The Authority's Advertising and Sponsorship Code sets out similar guidelines for the handling of advertising. In particular advertisements:

- must avoid offensive and profane language;
- should avoid salacious, violent or indecent themes, or sexual innuendo or stereotyping likely to cause serious offence;
- should avoid references to minority groups which are stereotypical, malicious, unkind or hurtful;
- should not include references to religious or political beliefs which are offensive, deprecating or hurtful – indeed the use of religious themes and treatments by non-religious groups should be treated with extreme care;
- should not demean or ridicule those who have physical, sensory or intellectual or mental health disabilities;
- show care in their handling of films, plays, music tracks or websites with salacious, violent or sexual themes;
- should not seek to use humour to circumvent the intention of the Code Rules.

■ This is one of a series of briefing papers produced by the Radio Authority for parliamentarians and policy makers. The full list of papers can be accessed at the ePolitix website (www.ePolitix.com/forum/radio-authority.htm) and at the Radio Authority's web site www.radioauthority.org.uk
© *Radio Authority*

Are the media now above the law?

Whilst privacy law dominates current media law debate, are we in danger of losing sight of how the media's power impacts on the law in other ways?

Article 10 of the European Convention on Human Rights (ECHR) provides that 'Everyone has the right to freedom of expression'. Until 1998, the courts viewed this principle merely as one of a number of considerations to be weighed in the balance of any judgment where it was relevant. In a string of cases decided in Strasbourg, it was held that English judges had been too parsimonious in according the right its due weight. By the time of the *Spycatcher* litigation, it had become clear that on this issue British justice was dancing to the beat of the wrong drum. Freedom of expression was an essential foundation of a democratic society, the media played the 'vital role of public watchdog'; they had a duty to impart information of public interest and the public had a right to receive it – these were considerations not to be swept aside with the glib and easy conscience evinced by the English judges. Incorporation of the ECHR by the Human Rights Act (HRA), it seemed, could not come too soon.

Since the Act, however, freedom of expression has at times seemed like a licence granted to the media to do whatever they like, however they like, to whomever they like. The media frenzy over the lives of the Soham murder defendants, Ian Huntley and Maxine Carr, reached such a pitch that the Attorney General felt forced to warn against the dangers of prejudicing a trial. The first trial of the Leeds United footballers Lee Bowyer and Jonathan Woodgate collapsed as a result of a report in the *Sunday Mirror*. In consequence, Lord Irvine announced plans to review the contempt of court laws accompanied by the early warning that self-regulation 'may not be sufficient on its own to deal with all cases which arise'. Among other

By Matthew Bradley

things, it seemed that the law was going to combat 'chequebook journalism'; the practice of paying jury members for their stories. Yet, in August 2002, the review was dropped after intense lobbying by the media and the Press Complaints Commission. Whilst the PCC did promise a tightening of its rules, it was clear that in this instance political concerns had overcome legislative needs. No government wants to rile the media if it can avoid it; it seemed that this consideration had prevailed over the demands of justice. But a pusillanimous legislature is not equivalent to a media above the law.

> *Freedom of expression has at times seemed like a licence granted to the media to do whatever they like, however they like, to whomever they like*

However, the jealously guarded power of the media to regulate itself appears in some respects to enable it to transcend the law. Whilst section 12 of the HRA means that all self-regulation in regard to privacy now arguably has statutory status, the risks of 'double jeopardy' arising from two punitive schemas, one administered by the courts, one by the regulatory bodies, seem exaggerated. 'Jeopardy' is an innocuous word in the context of the media's regulatory bodies. They cannot order the payment of

damages, nor prevent a broadcast or publication; their arsenal is restricted to investigation and the order to publish adjudications. Moreover, the need for the media to abide by their own rules is viewed by the PCC's erstwhile chairman Lord Wakeham as one without presumptive priority. That 'Editors think twice before breaching the code' is scant reassurance that the media take adequate heed of their responsibilities. The fact that he refers to the PCC's historic decisions as 'case law' further reinforces the impression that the press maintain a transcendental position vis-à-vis the law, and that they view themselves as doing so.

This transcendental role is not restricted to regulation; the media effectively play judge and jury in people's lives. In the case of John Leslie, the media usurped the law and levied their own sanctions; not damages, but the loss of his job and quite probably the hope of any future employment. Whilst sympathy for him may not be an immediate reaction, his plight amounts to a punishment achieved by a circumvention of all principles of natural justice. The fact that no charges have been brought against him is an indication of the scant likelihood of a successful conviction. Intrusions into people's private lives in the name of public interest often institute a similar process, as Dame Elizabeth Butler-Sloss' decision in *Venables v. News Group Newspapers* acknowledges. An injunction 'for life' against publication of details of the identities and whereabouts of the James Bulger killers was surely a humane and justifiable decision in light of the threats against their lives. This did not prevent furore in some sections of the media. The view was earnestly postulated that the use of bodyguards in this instance was preferable to any curtailment of freedom of expression. Such an ordering of priorities is nothing short of diabolical. Whilst public interest may be hard to define, it is possible to state when it is nowhere in sight.

The Venables case demonstrates that there are still balancing acts to be performed in relation to Article 10. In that case, Article 10 gave way to Article 2, the right to life, but the case is germane to the balancing act between Article 10 and Article 8 in the domain of privacy rights, without doubt the primary battleground of contemporary media law. In this area again, the legislature's reluctance to act seems to derive more from a placatory reverence for the media in an age of spin than from any assignable intent. In response, and perhaps to the legislators' relief, judges have increasingly seized upon Article 8 to expand pre-existing laws, in particular the law on breach of confidence, into laws giving effect to privacy claims. This of course has provoked media uproar over the presumptuous self-elevation of the judiciary. The media cannot have their cake and eat it; Article 10 has provided succour, but it also refers explicitly to the media's responsibilities; these responsibilities must include the duty to abide by Article 8. Nevertheless, for the sake of clarity in such a disputed area of law, and with no unified front as yet presented by the judiciary, the case for legislation in this area seems overwhelming.

The courts have not shrunk back from according other laws or principles priority over Article 10. Whilst the exceptions to Article 10(1) in 10(2) are to be construed strictly and Section 12 of the HRA stipulates that the public interest must be taken into account in proceedings relating to 'journalistic, literary or artistic material', the claims of such competing interests (those 'prescribed by law' and 'necessary in a democratic society') have not been quashed outright. The Shayler case demonstrates that certain legislation, in this case the Official Secrets Act, does not allow for any public interest defence at all, even where one could

be convincingly established. Statutes relating to harassment, sexual offences and copyright have all been used by parties in litigation to overcome arguments based on Article 10. Whilst the lapsed common law principle against prior restraint of publication was certainly given renewed vitality, Article 10 did not allow anything to be taken for granted. The refusal to lift an injunction in Imutran represents a harsh appraisal of a case with a convincing public interest element. *Ashworth and R v. Central Criminal Court, ex parte Bright, Alton and Rusbridger* shows that the Goodwin case did not vouchsafe the sacrosanct confidentiality of journalistic sources in all circumstances, especially those touching upon national security or relating to breaches of contractual confidentiality. Indeed, the House of Lords decision in *Punch* is indicative of a two-stage reaction by the judiciary to Article 10's in-corporation. After

initial exuberance by the Court of Appeal, the House of Lords had time to take stock. It is now clear that Article 10 cannot be used as a stick to batter all opposing considerations into submission; it just comes in Day-Glo packaging these days.

Freedom of expression is crucial to the maintenance of our democracy; incorporation of Article 10 must be welcomed but it is not the only pertinent factor in a discussion of the media's relationship to the law. Incorporation cannot of itself guarantee freedom of expression. Neither can a media uninhibited by all legal restraint. Consolidation of media ownership as dictated by market forces has not led to the most free of all possible markets where competition can play its role as 'best test of truth'. The fourth estate forms part of our democracy's cement, but it is also a global residency in which Rupert Murdoch plays with his toys. In 1995, when Tony Blair went to Hayman Island, Australia, to pay homage to News Corporation's executives, an indication was given as to the source of many of the current controversies in media law. As new information outlets proliferate, and as OFCOM prepares to take its first steps, it is nevertheless still optimistic to hope that legislators can view media law unclouded by political agendas.

■ This article first appeared in *The Telegraph*, 10 May 2003.

© *Matthew Bradley*

Freedom of expression is crucial to the maintenance of our democracy; incorporation of Article 10 must be welcomed but it is not the only pertinent factor in a discussion of the media's relationship to the law

---

KEY FACTS

■ There has been a significant increase in the number of people who regard television as their main source of world news: 79% in 2002, compared with 66% in 2001. By contrast, 9% of respondents named newspapers, down from 16% in 2001. (p 1)

■ Concerns about television standards in general, however, remain high – on a level with those observed in 2001, with 47% of respondents thinking standards had got worse (compared with 28% in 2000). (p 1)

■ A new cause for concern among respondents was the perception of intrusion into people's lives: 61% thought there was too much, making it a greater concern than too much sexual content (44%), swearing (56%) or violence (58%). (p 1)

■ When asked which source of news was most trusted (television, newspapers or radio), 70% named television. (p. 2)

■ Viewers continue to be concerned about quality and standards in general on television, with 47% of respondents thinking that programmes had got worse. (p. 2)

■ Most respondents (57%) said that they listened to the radio every day and 87% said they have not heard anything that offended them. (p. 3)

■ Internet access increased in 2002 to 52% of respondents (47% in 2001). (p. 3)

■ Eighty per cent of the parents believed that soaps did not promote positive images of the family, highlighting too many scenes of sex and violence, a high level of infidelity, alcohol abuse and an overall feeling of negativity as areas of concern. (p. 9)

■ British, Australian or American child will be exposed to 20,000-40,000 ads a year; American children spend 60 per cent more time in front of the TV screen each year than they do at school. (p. 11)

■ The majority of the population are quite positive towards advertising, but some feel that sometimes ads just go too far. (p. 14)

■ Just under a fifth of adults said that they had been personally offended by advertising they had seen in the past 12 months. (p. 14)

■ The Government is setting up a new super-regulator called the Office of Communications (OFCOM). It will swallow up separate regulators like the Independent Television Commission, the Radio Authority, the Office of Telecommunications and the Broadcasting Standards Commission. (p. 19)

■ There are 21 significant commercial radio owners, 70 overall, of 268 local and regional licences. (p. 21)

■ About 60% of people in the UK read a national daily paper, and 70% a national Sunday, but national newspaper sales have declined from the peak sales point of the late 1950s. The entire national press is owned by seven companies. The four largest of these account for about 90% of sales. (p. 24)

■ About Ofcom;
Ofcom is being designed to be a world-class regulator for the UK's converging communications sector. At the end of 2003, the new Office of Communications will merge the functions of five existing regulatory bodies: the Independent Television Commission (ITC), the Broadcasting Standards Commission (BSC), the Office of Telecommunications (Oftel), the Radio Authority (RAu) and the Radiocommunications Agency (RA). (p. 27)

■ The Press – newspapers and magazines – makes up the largest group of media. (p. 28)

■ Taking newspapers and magazines together, there are well over 10,000 different regular publications in the UK available to the advertiser. (p. 28)

■ There are now over 240 commercial stations, licensed and regulated by the Radio Authority, that pay for themselves by taking money from advertising. (p. 29)

■ The creation of a voluntary Press Council in 1953 heralded the beginning of press self-regulation. The aim was to maintain high ethical standards of journalism and to promote press freedom. (p. 30)

You might like to contact the following organisations for further information. Due to the increasing cost of postage, many organisations cannot respond to enquiries unless they receive a stamped, addressed envelope.

The Advertising Association
Abford House
15 Wilton Road
London, SW1V 1NJ
Tel: 020 7828 2771
Fax: 020 7931 0376
E-mail: aa@adassoc.org.uk
Web site: www.adassoc.org.uk
The Advertising Association is a federation of 25 trade bodies representing the advertising and promotional marketing industries including advertisers, agencies, media and support services.

Advertising Standards Authority (ASA)
Brook House, 2 Torrington Place
London, WC1E 7HW
Tel: 020 7580 5555
Fax: 020 7631 3051
E-mail: inquiries@asa.org.uk
Web site: www.asa.org.uk
The ASA is the independent, self-regulatory body for non-broadcast advertisements in the UK.

Broadcasting Standards Commission
5-8 The Sanctuary
London, SW1P 3JS
Tel: 020 7233 0544
Fax: 020 7233 0397
Web site: www.bsc.org.uk
The Broadcasting Standards Commission is the statutory body for standards and fairness in broadcasting.

Campaign for Press and Broadcasting Freedom (CPBF)
2nd Floor, Vi and Garner Smith House
23 Orford Road
Walthamstow
London, E17 9NL
Tel: 020 8521 5932
Fax: 020 8521 5932
E-mail: freepress@cpbf.org.uk
Web site: www.freepress.org.uk
Campaigns for more diverse, accessible and accountable media, and the right of reply for those suffering media distortion.

The English & Media Centre
18 Compton Terrace
London, N1 2UN
Tel: 020 7359 8080
Fax: 020 7354 0133
Web site:
www.englishandmedia.co.uk
Serves the needs of secondary and FE teachers and students of English and Media Studies in the UK.

Independent Television Commission (ITC)
33 Foley Street
London, W1W 7LT
Tel: 020 7306 7768
Fax: 020 7306 7737
Web site: www.itc.org.uk
The ITC licenses and regulates commercial television in the UK. Looks after viewers' interests by setting and maintaining the standards for programmes, advertising and technical quality.

Institute for Public Policy Research (IPPR)
30-32 Southampton Street
London, WC2E 7RA
Tel: 020 7470 6100
Fax: 020 7470 6111
E-mail: ippr@easynet.co.uk
Web site: www.ippr.org.uk
A left of centre think-tank.

mediawatch-uk
3 Willow House
Kennington Road
Ashford, TN24 0NR
Tel: 01233 633936
Fax: 01233-633836
E-mail: info@mediawatchuk.org
Web site: www.mediawatchuk.org/mainsite.htm
mediawatch-uk provides an independent voice for those concerned about issues of taste and decency in the media.

National Family and Parenting Institute (NFPI)
430 Highgate Studios
58-79 Highgate Road
London, NW5 1TL
Tel: 020 7424 3460
Fax: 020 7424 3590
E-mail: info@nfpi.org
Web site: www.nfpi.org and
An independent charity working to improve the lives of parents and families by campaigning for a more family-friendly society.

Ofcom
Office of Communications
Riverside House, 2a Southwark Bridge Road, London, SE1 9HA
Tel: 020 7981 3000
Fax: 020 7981 3333
E-mail: enq@ofcom.org.uk
Web site: www.ofcom.org.uk
Ofcom will be the new regulatory body for the UK communications sector.

Press Complaints Commission
1 Salisbury Square
London, EC4Y 8JB
Tel: 020 7353 1248
Fax: 020 7353 8355
pcc@pcc.org.uk
Web site: www.pcc.org.uk
The PCC is an independent body which deals with complaints from members of the public about editorial content in newspapers and magazines. Helpline: 020 7353 3732. Scottish Help Line: 0131 220 6652

Radio Authority
Holbrook House
14 Great Queen Street
London, WC2B 5DG
Tel: 020 7430 2724
Fax: 020 7405 7062
Web site:
www.radioauthority.org.uk
The Radio Authority licenses and regulates independent radio in accordance with the statutory requirements of the Broadcasting Acts 1990 and 1996.

ACKNOWLEDGEMENTS

The publisher is grateful for permission to reproduce the following material.

While every care has been taken to trace and acknowledge copyright, the publisher tenders its apology for any accidental infringement or where copyright has proved untraceable. The publisher would be pleased to come to a suitable arrangement in any such case with the rightful owner.

Chapter One: Social Effects

The public's view, © Broadcasting Standards Commission/Independent Television Commission, *Uses of the media*, © BBC, ITC, Independent Committee for the Supervision of Standards of Telephone Information Services, ITC, Institute for Public Policy Research and The Radio Authority, *TV taste and decency in decline, say viewers*, © Telegraph Group Limited, London 2003, *Children's TV*, © Broadcasting Standards Commission/ Independent Television Commission, *Top children's television programmes*, © Broadcasting Standards Commission/Independent Television Commission, *Bleak television landscape*, © Telegraph Group Limited, London 2003, *Getting into a lather*, © NFPI, *Gun culture on TV*, © mediawatch-uk, *BBC to provide more warnings of adult content*, © Guardian Newspapers Limited 2003, *A brand new kind of advert*, © Guardian Newspapers Limited 2003, *Equipment in eldest child's bedroom*, © Independent Television Commission/Broadcasting Standards Commission, *Children and advertising*, © Advertising Standards Authority (ASA), *Serious offence in non-broadcast advertising*, © Advertising Standards Authority (ASA), *Offence in advertising*, © Advertising Standards Authority (ASA).

Chapter Two: Regulation and Ownership

Cracking the Communications Bill, © English and Media Centre, *Why the Communications Bill is bad news*, © Campaign for Press and Broadcasting Freedom (CPBF), *The prime targets*, © Guardian Newspapers Limited 2003, *UK media ownership*, © European Federation of Journalists, *Media ownership* © Crown copyright is reproduced with the permission of Her Majesty's Stationery Office, *TV ad rules to be relaxed this year, says Ofcom chief*, © Guardian Newspapers Limited 2003, *Ofcom*, © Ofcom, *The advertising media*, © The Advertising Association, *Press self-regulation*, © Press Complaints Commission, *Frequently asked questions by students answered*, © Press Complaints Commission, *Complaints about teenage magazines* © The Teenage Magazine Arbitration Panel (TMAP), *Privacy law is 'best way' to protect the public*, © Telegraph Group Limited, London 2003, *Privacy law*, © Institute for Public Policy Research (IPPR), *Taste and decency*, © Radio Authority, *Are the media now above the law?*, © Matthew Bradley.

Photographs and illustrations:

Pages 1, 4, 13, 19, 32, 39: Simon Kneebone; pages 8, 16, 35: Bev Aisbett; pages 10, 26, 36: Pumpkin House.

Craig Donnellan
Cambridge
September, 2003